Torah in Motion Creating Dance Midrash

Torah in Motion Creating Dance Midrash

JoAnne Tucker
Susan Freeman

INTEGRATED MEDIA
NEW YORK

All rights reserved, including without limitation the right to reproduce this book or any portion thereof in any form or by any means, whether electronic or mechanical, now known or hereinafter invented, without the express written permission of the publisher.

Copyright © 1990 by JoAnne Tucker, Susan Freeman

ISBN 978-1-4976-4877-7

This edition published in 2014 by Open Road Integrated Media, Inc.
345 Hudson Street
New York, NY 10014
www.openroadmedia.com

Limbs and tongue and heart and mind shall join to praise Your Name.
(From the Sabbath liturgy)

Table of Contents

Foreword — *xiii*
Preface — *xv*
Introduction — *xix*

Genesis

Light from Darkness (1:4)	3
Fill the Earth (1:28)	5
First Shabbat (2:2)	7
Naming the Creatures (2:19)	9
Discovery (3:7)	11
Bursting of the Floodgates (7:11-12)	13
Gibberish (11:9)	15
Abram, Go Forth (12:1)	17
Sister . . . Let Me Live! (12:13)	19
Sarah Laughed (18:12)	21
Lot's Wife (19:26)	23
Hagar's Eyes Are Opened (21:19)	25
The Binding of Isaac (22:1, 22:7, 22:11)	27
Sarah's Lifetime (23:1)	29
Rebekah's Veil (24:65)	32

Jacob Emerges (25:26)	34
Jacob: One Who Disguises (27:19)	36
Jacob's Dream (28:12)	39
Jacob's Journey Continues (29:1)	41
Sisters: Leah and Rachel (29:17)	43
Jacob Wrestles (32:25)	45
Dinah (34:1)	47
Isaac Dies (35:28-29)	50
Joseph Dreams (37:7)	52
Joseph Is Cast into the Pit (37:23-24)	54
Judah's Pledge to Tamar (38:18)	56
Joseph in Charge (41:45)	58
Joseph Names His Sons (41:51-52)	60
Egyptians Become Serfs (47:25)	63
Blessing Ephraim & Manasseh (48:20)	65
Joseph Mourns His Father (50:10)	68

Exodus

A New Pharaoh Deals Harshly (1:10)	73
The Burning Bush (3:2)	76
Moses Stands on Holy Ground (3:5)	78
Let My People Go (5:1)	80
Moses' Impediment (6:12)	82
Frogs Everywhere (8:2)	85

Darkness Descends on Egypt (10:22)	87
Leaving Egypt (12:11)	89
Sign and Symbol of Freedom (13:16)	92
Crossing the Sea (14:22)	94
Hands of Victory (17:11)	96
Keep the Sabbath (20:8)	98
Amazement at Sinai (20:15)	100
Helping Your Enemy (23:5)	102
Against Cruelty (23:19)	105
Giving (25:1-2)	107
Winged Cherubim (25:20)	109
Colored Gate (27:16)	111
Anointment (29:7)	113
The Lure of Gold (32:2-3)	115
Moses Sees the Golden Calf (32:19)	117
God Shields Moses (33:21-22)	119
Excellence for the Tabernacle (36:2)	121
Levels of Sacred Space (40:30-32)	123
The Cloud and God's Presence (40:34-35)	125

Leviticus

An Offering By Fire (1:17)	129
Drawing Near (2:1)	131
Holy on Contact (6:11)	133

Blood Ritual (8:23)	136
They Saw and Shouted (9:24)	138
Unclean! Unclean! (13:45)	140
Contaminated Fabric (13:47)	142
A Plague in the House (14:37-38)	144
Scapegoat (16:21)	146
Defiling the Land (18:28)	148
Leave Some for the Poor (19:9-10)	150
Stumbling Blocks (19:14)	152
Love the Stranger (19:34)	154
Etrog, Palm, Myrtle, & Willow (23:40)	156
Sound the Shofar (25:9)	159
The Jubilee Year (25:10)	161
Reward and Punishment (26:3-4)	163
Clearing Out the Old (26:10)	166

Numbers

In the Wilderness (1:1)	171
Blessing of Peace (6:26)	173
Shouldering the Sacred (7:9)	175
The Wave (8:11)	177
Miriam Stricken (12:10)	179
Fringed Reminder (15:39)	181
Moses Hears and Falls (16:4)	183

Striking the Rock (20:11)	185
Copper Serpent (21:9)	187
Balaam Blesses (24:5)	189
Flaunting Leads to Death (25:6)	191
Daughters of Zelophehad (27:1)	193
New Moons (28:11)	195
Limits of Women's Vows (30:6)	197
Cities of Refuge (35:11)	200

Deuteronomy

Moses' Final Address (1:1)	205
Honor Father and Mother (5:16)	207
Hear, O Israel (6:4)	209
Teach With All Your Heart (6:6-7)	212
The Hornets (7:25)	214
Open Your Heart (10:16)	216
Path to the Appointed Site (12:5)	218
Sweep Out Evil (13:6)	220
Do Not Deviate (17:11)	222
Protecting Trees During War (20:19)	224
Regard for Animals (22:6-7)	226
Land of Milk and Honey (26:9)	228
A Holy People (28:9-10)	230
Return to God (30:10)	232

God's Hidden Countenance (31:17)	234
Like an Eagle (32:11)	236
Israel: Fat and Kicked (32:15)	238
God's Everlasting Arms (33:27)	240
Moses Sees the Promised Land (34:3)	243
Appendix I Holidays and Life Events: Suggested Dance Midrashim	245
Appendix II Resources for Leading Sessions	248
Appendix III How To Ask Questions	250
Appendix IV Dance Midrashim by Torah Portion	253
Bibliography	
Sources Related to Midrash	259
Sources Related to Dance	262

Foreword

It is safe to say that most Jewish adults do not take the Bible seriously, viewing it as a myth of the Ancient Near East with little relevance to our modern context. At best, exposure to the Bible comes at a Friday evening or Saturday morning service when the biblical weekly portion is "read to" or "preached at" them. Lay people simply are rarely asked to grapple actively with the sacred stories of our tradition and therefore have a difficult time recognizing their power to shape priorities and life direction.

Yet, enmeshed in a secular culture which seems void of ultimate values and living at a time when life choices are most frequently shaped by the pursuit of the material, we who search for a taste of the holy are compelled to immerse ourselves in the totality of our religious tradition and to read the Bible, the core of that tradition, more seriously. By intimately confronting the biblical text and allowing it to resonate within our souls, we, like the Rabbis of old, can begin to learn about ourselves as Jews and as human beings.

If only we would avail ourselves of the process of Midrash, the attempt to search out meaning from the Bible by listening closely to its every word, and by attending to all its nuances and symbolism, then the text would come alive for us and the characters would speak to us. By opening ourselves to the

Foreword

sacred stories of our tradition in which the characters are multi-dimensional and appear in life situations very much akin to our own, we will be touched and transformed.

The key is to become totally engaged with the text. Meaning will occur for us when we are active respondents who are stimulated both by what is recorded in the text as well as by what is omitted. As we imaginatively fill in textual gaps and ponder the complexities of motive and the ambiguities of character, a multitude of interpretations are created.

Furthermore, the recreation of biblical scenes and characters by the sensitive respondent can take many different artistic forms: writing, music, drama, visual art, and dance. In recent years, all these aesthetic media have been used to bring life to the biblical text in new and creative Midrashic ways. However, there is not a more dynamic art form by which to interpret the Bible than dance. The latent power of any narrative and the often complex human interaction included in it can most vividly be captured by the movement and creative spontaneity of modern dance.

This guide to leading Dance Midrash, which helps the modern Jew both to approach the biblical text Midrashically and then to translate the resultant interpretations into meaningful improvisations and choreography, adds a new link to the wonderful chain of Jewish interpretative tradition. I hope it will be used by scores of religious school teachers, camp counselors, and adult education programmers, and thereby touch the lives of innumerable Jewish young people and adults. I am proud to associate myself with its vision and with the creativity of its writers.

Rabbi Norman J. Cohen
Hebrew Union College
Jewish Institute of Religion
New York, New York

Preface

The Development of Dance Midrash

The idea for developing a form of expression called "Dance Midrash" grew out of a combination of events. In 1981, JoAnne Tucker, working with Richard Jacobs, then a Rabbinic student and dancer, created a dance piece *M'Vakshei Or* for The Avodah Dance Ensemble. The Avodah Dance Ensemble, directed by Dr. Tucker, is a professional New York based modern dance company which creates repertory inspired by Jewish ritual, liturgy, and history. *M'vakshei Or* was inspired by rituals that are part of the Torah service. The middle section of the piece evolved into an improvisation based on a verse from the weekly Torah portion. As *M'Vakshei Or* was being rehearsed and performed, the dancers and JoAnne began referring to these improvisations as Dance Midrashim.

In 1986 Rabbi Norman Cohen, Professor of Midrash and Dean of the Hebrew Union College-Jewish Institute of Religion in New York, led a workshop for a new group of Avodah dancers during which he explicated the process he uses in developing Midrash. These ideas were incorporated into the dance improvisations.

Preface

When Susan Freeman, then a Rabbinic student at HUC-JIR, joined the company in the winter of 1988, she added new enthusiasm to the process. She and JoAnne Tucker began pushing the improvisations further with the enthusiastic cooperation of Avodah dancers Kezia Gleckman, Deborah Hanna, and Beth Bardin who, in turn, also played an active role in developing the ideas from which this book began to take form.

Drawing on her teaching experience at Jewish religious school and camp, Susan saw the potential expansion of these improvisations into a format that teachers could use in the classroom. Together, JoAnne and Susan evolved a format that is suitable for different age groups in a variety of settings. The Dance Midrashim in this book combine elements of movement and teaching techniques with the traditional Midrashic process of explaining and elaborating on Torah text.

Acknowledgements

We would like to express appreciation to those who gave so generously of themselves in helping with the development of Dance Midrash.

Dr. Walter Jacob, Rabbi of Rodef Shalom Congregation in Pittsburgh, Pennsylvania, and Mr. and Mrs. Theodore Baumritter of Boca Raton, Florida, provided the funding for *M'Vakshei Or*, the dance work which led to the development of the concept.

The Board of Directors of the Avodah Dance Ensemble consistently encouraged and guided the development of modern dance in a Jewish context.

The dancers of The Avodah Dance Ensemble, throughout the decade of the 1980s, have enthusiastically given of themselves, creatively wrestling with text and performing inspiring and impressive Dance Midrash improvisations.

Rabbi Richard Jacobs of Brooklyn Heights Synagogue, friend and fellow artist, helped to guide the early development of the process and improvisations while a dancer with Avodah from 1981 to 1986.

Rabbi Norman Cohen has been a source of inspiration and guidance on our journey, always encouraging our endeavors.

We wish to acknowledge the fine contribution to this work by Tom Brazil, photographer.

Preface

Hebrew Union College-Jewish Institute of Religion and Brooklyn Heights Synagogue provided space for the photographic sessions. The teachers and students in the preschool, Grade 5, Grade 8, and Senior Adult group from the synagogue contributed their time and energy through their participation in the photography sessions. Ellen Robbins, an outstanding modern dance teacher, generously entrusted her talented students to us, helping us to illustrate a variety of Dance Midrashim.

Deborah Marcus brought several senior adults to one of the photography sessions. A special thanks to all of these individuals.

We deeply appreciate the encouragement, support, and enthusiasm of our editors/publishers, Audrey Friedman Marcus and Rabbi Raymond A. Zwerin.

Finally, we are grateful to our families who have given us so much love and support over the years. JoAnne's family: Janet, Leonard (may his memory be for a blessing), Julie, and Rachel, and JoAnne's dear friend Murray. Susan's family: Sam, Joyce, Laura, Carol, and Phil.

Preface to Fall 2000 Edition

It has been 10 years since **Torah In Motion: Creating Dance Midrash** first appeared in print. Since that time we have continued our exploration of movement as an important tool in religious education both in leading sessions ourselves and in training others to use the technique. It is exciting to see how the field is growing! We are most appreciative of the dancers, educators, and clergy who continue to contribute to our learning and who enthusiastically welcome improvisational movement into their work as a way to understand sacred text.

We want to thank "E-Reads.com" for making **Torah In Motion: Creating Dance Midrash** again available. In particular we want to acknowledge Richard Curtis, President. Amy Meo and Jennifer Hackworth's care in handling the details of the republication is very much appreciated.

We thank Tom Brazil, photographer and Rabbi Raymond Zwerin and Audrey Friedman Marcus of A.R.E. Publishing, Inc., original publishers of **Torah in Motion: Creating Dance Midrash,** for graciously permitting us to use the original photo and cover design.

Introduction

Through the ages, the Bible has served as a constant source for choreographers. While a number of books, especially in religious education, have chapters or sections devoted to such dance, no other book draws on a Midrashic interpretation of the Five Books of Moses (Torah) as a model for structuring movement activities.

WHAT IS MIDRASH

The word Midrash (Midrashim, plural) is derived from the Hebrew, meaning to explain, to interpret, to search, or to seek out. The Bible is written in a terse style, eschewing details, leaving gaps in conversations and events. Midrash is an intellectual process which fills in those gaps by raising questions elicited from the text and then answering them. The jumping off point for creating a literary Midrash is usually a word or phrase from the biblical text. A Midrash may then elaborate; clarify; link disparate people, places, events, or objects; relate the biblical texts to contemporary issues; explicate a Jewish value; identify a theme; make a play on words.

Midrashic literature has its origins with the Rabbis of the first centuries of the common era. While it reaches its zenith as an intellectual, literary process in about the 8th century, its continuous development can be traced even to this day.

Introduction

Midrashim are written in a variety of styles—terse, embellished, straightforward, or symbolic. They may follow the text closely or go off on various tangents. Since it is not within the purview of this introduction to define Midrash as such, and since volumes have been written about Midrash, you are referred to the bibliography for a list of readings on the subject.

WHAT IS DANCE MIDRASH

By asking pertinent questions and then answering them, Midrash brings the Bible to life. By making connections between the biblical text and its times and the modern reader, Midrash enables the Bible to become more immediate and relevant. Dance Midrash is a new genre which has its roots in the tradition of interpreting biblical texts. Dance Midrash is a form of interpreting the text through movement activities which illustrate and explicate the nuances of verses under consideration.

While literary Midrash is specifically an intellectual endeavor, Dance Midrash is mainly physical—the former employs the mind, the latter the body and the mind. Dance enables us to interact closely with one another, thus heightening the social response and deepening the emotional experience. As we engage in dance movements, we increase mutual understanding and awareness. Through dance, we enhance our identification with the different times, places, and/or personalities encountered in the biblical text. Moreover, since texts can be experienced on a multiplicity of levels, dance can be a significant aid in fostering retention of learning.

The movement activities in this book challenge dancers to approach and make connections with texts that may at first seem remote. Each Dance Midrash requires participants to deal with the text itself; to reflect on and wrestle with ideas and values in verses drawn from the Five Books of Moses (Torah); and to put the text into a broader context by analyzing these ideas and values as they impact on world values, social consciousness, community and interpersonal interactions, and on our own personal growth.

THE MIDRASH PROCESS

Rabbi Norman Cohen, scholar of Midrash, has outlined the following six steps which are useful in understanding how written Midrash is created, and which have also influenced the development of Dance Midrash.
1. Have each individual read the biblical text silently and slowly, paying attention to every detail. Then, in a group, read a small portion of the text out loud.
2. Pay attention to both the black and the white (black referring to what is written and white to what is not written or to what might be implied).

Introduction

3. Ask difficult humanistic questions, particularly questions which might fill in the gaps regarding emotions felt by a biblical character. Look at how the lives of these characters parallel our own.
4. Look at the story (or the biblical moment) from other points of view, especially those of characters who don't speak and of inanimate objects.
5. Isolate one moment. Look at the dynamics of that moment—what is happening, what change is taking place, what aspects of a relationship will now never be the same, etc.
6. Take into consideration the larger narrative and how the moment or story fits into the total picture. Focus on the unity of Torah (how the moment relates to past moments or foreshadows events to come). See how the whole informs the parts and vice versa. (Appendix III may prove helpful in facilitating discussions. It provides guidance in the techniques of how to ask questions related to the biblical verse and how to take the biblical verse one step further.)

Refer to these six steps when preparing a text for use in creating Dance Midrash. Focusing on one of the steps with the participants can also enrich such a session.

ORGANIZATION OF THIS BOOK

Torah in Motion: Creating Dance Midrash contains dance activities for over 100 specific passages of the Torah. Each of these passages and its concomitant activities appear on a double page spread. The features of each of these spreads are as follows:

At the top left-hand side is the name of the book of the Torah from which the verse is taken.

Immediately below the name of the book of the Torah is the assessed level of difficulty for the movement activity contained in that chapter—beginner, intermediate, advanced.

The title of the chapter comes next, and is followed by the verse from Torah on which the movement activities are based.

Five sections then follow:

1. Description—an explication of the passage explaining its meaning and/or putting it into the biblical context. This may include who is speaking, where the action is taking place, when, what came before, what comes after, and/or relevant contemporary material.
2. Motivating Movement—a warm-up exercise which focuses on movement itself, rather than on the context and cognitive ideas in the verse. These movements are insinuated from the Torah passage

Introduction

and, in turn, prepare the participants for the Dance Midrash and the Challenge.
3. Dance Midrash—a clearly defined dance improvisation (or occasionally choreographed movement) through which dancers expand upon, explore, and/or bring the biblical verse into perspective.
4. Making Connections—questions and discussion ideas which touch on one or more of the following: the meaning of the Torah verse then and now, how the ideas in the verse relate to the contemporary world, how the ideas relate to the participant. (This section is sometimes placed before the Dance Midrash.)
5. Challenge—a concluding dance activity that will engage the participants' intellect, creativity, and physical energies on a more advanced level. On occasion, a leader may choose to do the Challenge prior to or instead of the Dance Midrash.

At the end of the book are four Appendixes. In Appendix I the Dance Midrashim are categorized according to holidays and life cycle events. In Appendix IV they are categorized according to the Torah portion in which each verse appears. Appendix II contains resources for leading sessions, and Appendix III provides guidelines on how to ask questions.

Note: Although Dance Midrash exercises appear in the book in the order of the Torah portions, there are other ways to draw upon them, depending on the needs of the teaching situation. Most notably, some of the exercises can be used for teaching holidays and life cycle events (see Appendix I).

THE LEADER
Characteristics

It is clear by now that Dance Midrash is a new use of dance and a new way to study Torah. Therefore, there are certain qualifications for leaders of Dance Midrash. Ideally, the leader should have had exposure to modern dance and be an ongoing student of Torah. Few of us have expertise in either of these areas, let alone in both of them. Therefore, a willingness to learn more about Torah, along with good energy, personal enthusiasm, and a pioneering spirit are the important qualities for a leader of this new learning technique.

Prior to leading a session, the leader should read several chapters before and after the biblical verse, or read the entire weekly portion in which the verse appears. (In synagogues throughout the world, the Torah is read in fifty-four weekly portions. Each portion is called a *sedra*. There are anywhere from one to five Dance Midrashim for each *sedra*. See Appendix IV for a listing of Dance Midrashim by *sedra*.)

Additionally, the leader may wish to read different translations of the Bible to detect nuances in meaning. If possible, read the verses in Hebrew and look for the subtle word associations and/or study written Midrashim related to the verses. It would also be enriching to participate in a weekly Torah study group at a local synagogue or Jewish Community Center.

A leader who is a beginning dancer might want to seek out a class in modern dance technique, creative movement, or movement improvisation.

Models of Leadership

There are essentially two models of leadership: leader as participant who teaches by demonstrating, or leader as active observer who teaches by providing feedback. Each model has advantages and disadvantages. Therefore, a leader may want to switch back and forth between the models. The following questions will help the leader decide on when to dance and when to watch.

Breaking the Ice/Giving Permission—What role best allows me to help participants get over shyness or inhibitions?

Demonstration or Discovery—Will participants get more out of seeing movement demonstrated so that they can visualize one or more possibilities, or will they get more out of verbal coaching so that the discovery of movement possibilities is left solely to them?

Motivation—What will help energize, inspire, and challenge the group most, my participation or my observations?

Feedback—Will my experience with the group or my observation of the whole picture allow me to give the most specific and helpful feedback?

Safety—If safety is a concern, what role allows me best to ensure it?

Finally, a leader will need to prioritize the considerations, weighing whether answers to some of the above questions are of higher priority than others. (For example, if safety is a big concern, and the leader feels it can best be ensured by keeping an eye on the whole picture, he/she will choose to be an active observer rather than a participant.)

Leader Creativity

A good leader also seeks a creative approach to leading the sessions. Creativity is the act of inventing something new or expressing something in a new way. The following suggestions may help in establishing the creative spark.

Ask lots of questions in a variety of different ways (see Appendix III for specific examples).

Become involved with the activities—demonstrate the obvious or outrageous and actively and energetically coach the dancers.

Experiment with expressing things in new ways, such as juxtaposing what might seem to clash (i.e., drums accompanying fluid movement).

Brainstorm—see how many different ideas the group can come up with given one specific situation or problem.

Elaborate on an idea—see how far the group can take a given idea.

Encourage more advanced and original work to develop by reinforcing positive creative behavior. Some ways to do this are to notice what the participants are doing, to encourage spontaneity, to welcome an incomplete idea (this may spark others' ideas and give clarification to the original idea), and to respond to suggestions with a non-judgmental attitude.

TERMS USED IN THIS BOOK

Most of the language used in describing exercises in this book will be familiar, suggesting actions and ways of dancing that are easy for the leader to facilitate and for the group to follow. Specific ideas for stimulating creative movement, such as verbal images, physical objects, and suggestions of sounds, are included in Appendix II.

However, there are also some technical dance terms and concepts used in this book. The leader may want to become familiar with the following terms:

Improvisation—spontaneous movement based on a specific set of instructions

Choreography—a given sequence of movements which can be repeated

Quality of Movement—the predominant characteristic of the movement; there are six basic qualities, the first four of which are drawn from *Dance, A Creative Art Experience* by Margaret N. H'Doubler (Madison, WI: University of Wisconsin Press, 1966):

Staccato—short, quick and sharp movement

Sustained—continuous slow movement

Percussive—strong forceful movement

Swinging—movement which goes back and forth or side to side in an even rhythm

Bound—limited and tense movement in which the limbs of the body are close to the center of the body

Open—flowing movement in which the limbs move out from the center of the body

Rhythm—a recurring pattern, usually with an underlying steady beat, to which there are accents

Tempo—how fast or slow the underlying beat is

Introduction

Phrase—in dance terms a natural rhythm of the body like breathing or a heart beat, or a specified number of beats with given accents

Space—the amount of space used (i.e., moving in place, in a small area, or covering the entire available space). Also, how the body moves through a given area. This includes:

Direction—forward, backward, sideways, diagonal

Pattern—such as a circle, straight line or zigzag

Level—moving on the ground (i.e., sitting or crawling); close to the ground; standing level; on relevé or tip toes; or off the ground (i.e., leaping, lifted up).

Shape—the predominant design the body makes while moving (i.e., round, curved, straight, angular, or like a familiar object or pattern)

Dynamic—the amount of change and contrast that occurs in a movement phrase or a series of phrases

Refer to this section and review the definitions of appropriate terms when planning a Dance Midrash. By focusing on the aspects of dance outlined here, the leader can be more precise in his/her coaching and feedback to the group.

LEVELS OF DIFFICULTY

The suggestions provided in this section are meant to serve as a guide. Each leader is encouraged to modify them based on his/her needs.

Each exercise indicates a suggested level: beginner, intermediate, or advanced. Despite these indications, exercises can be adapted for different needs. For example, a short section of an advanced exercise might be adapted for a younger or less experienced group. Or, an advanced group might explore more thoroughly and intricately a Dance Midrash or a Challenge presented in an exercise marked "beginner." In general, however, the assignment of levels is based on these guidelines:

Beginner—This dance material is more concrete and straightforward; ideas are less complicated and/or less sophisticated. The exercises are most readily appropriate for less experienced dancers of all ages, groups of mixed ages and levels, and children in preschool through Grade 6.

Intermediate—Dance material here is more difficult; ideas require greater sophistication. These exercises are most readily appropriate for dancers with some experience, junior high school to senior adults, and more experienced groups of mixed ages and levels.

Advanced—For the dance material in this category, prior dance experience will be helpful. Ideas in these sections are the most sophisticated and

Introduction

challenging. These exercises are appropriate for experienced dancers, teenagers, and adults.

HOW TO PROCEED

The guidelines that follow suggest an ideal way to approach leading a session. The leader should adapt these guidelines according to his/her own needs and experience.

1. Choose Exercise Prior to Session
   a. Read and think about the Torah portion from which the exercise comes.
   b. Apply Norman Cohen's steps as outlined on page xiv of this Introduction.
   c. Think about coaching strategies and questions to ask. Refer to Appendix III on page 241.
2. Beginning the Session—Two Possibilities
   a. Follow the suggestions outlined in the Motivating Movement section.
   b. Read the passage from Torah and describe the scene.
3. The Next Step
   a. If you began with movement, now describe the scene.
   b. If you described the scene, go to Motivating Movement.
   c. If you have described the scene, but don't feel the group is ready to move, go to the "Making Connections" section.
4. Dance Midrash
   a. State the improvisation clearly.
   b. Have the group dance several minutes or longer based on attention span.
5. Making Connections
   a. Ask questions as specified.
   b. Elaborate on the discussion if desired. (For help on questioning, see Appendix III on page 241.
6. Evaluate the Improvisation
   a. Ask for feedback, feelings, reactions and new ideas.
   b. Start with positive comments.
   c. Proceed to what could be done to make the improvisation better.
7. Based on Feedback
   a. Dance the improvisation again.
8. Optional
   a. Present the Challenge.

SETTINGS

Dance Midrash can be used in a variety of settings. The following mix-and-match table might trigger creative ideas for settings in which to incorporate Dance Midrash.

Introduction

Who Can Lead?	*Where?*	*When?*
Religious school teachers	Religious schools	Classes
Day school teachers	Day schools	Assemblies
Rabbis	Colleges	Services
Cantors	Camps	Sermons
Song leaders	Community Centers	Holiday celebrations
Camp counselors	Senior adult homes	*Havurah* meetings
Youth group leaders	Dance studios	
Youth group members	Adult education programs	
Programmers	Special performances	
Dance teachers	Retreats	
Family members		

THE PHYSICAL SPACE

Ideally, the dance space should be somewhere between the size of a large, empty classroom and the size of half a basketball court. In addition to the classroom, possible sites are an outdoor space in which boundaries have been defined, a stage, a pulpit area, or a social hall. If space is limited, do one or more of the following:

Rearrange furniture and other objects.

Have small groups improvise while the others watch, then switch.

Choose a Dance Midrash which can be done using less "traveling" and more movement in place.

GROUP SIZE

Ideally, a group should have 4 to 30 participants. Dance Midrashim may be adapted for groups of any size. For example, three dancers who want to choreograph a trio might look for a Dance Midrash which divides a larger group into groups of three. They can then choreograph a dance based on that Dance Midrash idea. For a larger group, a congregation or the like, choose a Dance Midrash (or section) which can be done in place, primarily using the upper body.

CONCLUSION

Dance Midrash is a new and exciting way to approach the Bible. As movement is merged with the structure and style of Midrash, participants will wrest new meaning from the biblical text.

This Introduction describes all the skills and tools necessary to introduce Dance Midrash to a group. By drawing on the material in this book, a leader

Introduction

can engage people of every age in an exciting and satisfying process. Imaginations will be triggered and, in a playful and fun-filled manner, participants will discover new insights into the Torah. It won't be long before such comments as the following are heard: "I never would have thought about the passage this way unless I danced it!"

Torah in Motion
Creating Dance Midrash

Genesis

Genesis
Beginner ■ ☐ ☐

Light from Darkness

And God separated the light from the darkness. (Genesis 1:4)

Description

The Torah begins with the description of creation. Amidst the darkness all around, God said, "Let there be light," and there was light. God saw that the light was good, and separated the light from the darkness.

Motivating Movement

1. Have dancers improvise on images of light:
    a. Ask dancers to be bolts of lightning. Have them take turns "bolting" across the room. Coach them to pay special attention to the design lightning makes as it zigzags in the sky. Ask them to create clear spatial patterns as they go across the room. They should be able to draw the pattern they make.
    b. Have each dancer portray a small spark that grows in intensity. Begin in a tight ball on the floor and grow steadily, bigger, stronger, and brighter.
2. Have dancers improvise on separation:

a. Have the group begin in, and then move out of, a designated part of the room. Encourage them to move away with the intent of separating from the space with great effort and care.

Dance Midrash

Before the creation of light, "the earth was unformed and void, with darkness over the surface of the deep and a wind from God sweeping over the water" (Genesis 1:2). Have the dancers imagine they are light being created amidst the darkness. Experiment in different ways with light being created: quickly in one burst and slowly, as a growing spark. End with the group coming together to form a large mass of light distinguishing itself from its surroundings.

Making Connections

God created the light, saw that it was good, and called the light day. What then do we make of the darkness, the darkness called night? God doesn't call the darkness good, but neither is darkness called bad. Maybe darkness is defined by how we perceive it. Have the group share how they perceive darkness, and perhaps dance these perceptions.

Challenge

The group imagines that throughout the seven days of creation, light and darkness are negotiating how many hours of the day each should rule. Divide the group: one half is light, the other is darkness. Dance this dialogue of negotiation. To further develop this improvisation, have the dancers keep in mind what day of creation it is and what is being created on that day. For example, do they negotiate differently on the sixth day when male and female are created as compared to the seventh day when God blesses the day and rests?

Genesis
Intermediate ■ ■ □

Fill the Earth

God blessed them and God said to them, "Be fertile and increase, fill the earth and master it." (Genesis 1:28)

Description

God instructs Adam and Eve that it is a blessing to have children.

Motivating Movement

1. The dancers begin on one side of the room and zigzag across the space. The goal is to cover as much space as they can in as few big movements as possible.
2. The dancers stand in a circle. One dancer imagines holding and blessing a baby. That dancer then hands the imaginary baby to the next dancer in a way that suggests a continuation of the blessing—giving another an opportunity to bless the baby. The next dancers continue this pattern of blessing.

Dance Midrash

Each dancer creates a blessing that consists of four movement phrases which are bold and expansive, yet nurturing. The themes of the blessing phrases are:

May you be fertile
Increase
Fill the earth
Master the earth

Making Connections

Human beings are intended to be a blessing to God; so, too, are children intended to be a blessing to their parents. Talk about how children you know (your own, siblings, cousins, or children or siblings of a friend) bring blessings to the world.

Challenge

In Genesis 1:28 raising children and mastering the earth are linked. Have dancers choose three qualities needed in order to raise children to be part of a "blessed earth." The dancers, working either individually or in pairs, create a dance which expresses the three qualities. They perform their dances in front of the rest of the group. The group then gives the performers feedback on what qualities they observed. The performers rework their dances based on the feedback they received, trying to refine their movements to express precisely the qualities they have chosen. Examples of qualities include: love, respect, discipline, sense of humor, faith, kindness.

Genesis
Beginner ■ □ □

First Shabbat

On the seventh day God finished the work which God had begun doing, and God ceased on the seventh day from all the work which God had done. (Genesis 2:2)

Description

After six days of creating, God rested on the seventh day, Shabbat. We are commanded to observe and remember the seventh day and make it holy.

Motivating Movement

1. Have the group begin by clapping six counts and holding the seventh count. When the pattern is clearly established, have the group walk the pattern. Continue by coaching participants to experiment with moving different parts of their bodies on the six counts, still holding on the seventh count. As a final step for older and advanced groups, see if the group can maintain the rhythmic pattern when no one is counting out loud.
2. Have the group experiment with restful movement of a sustained nature on the seventh count in contrast to a total stop or rest.

Making Connections

Ask participants what the experience in the previous section tells them about observing Shabbat, the day of rest. Was it easy or difficult to rest on the seventh count? Did they use the sixth count to prepare for the seventh count? How do they prepare for Shabbat on Thursday night or Friday?

Dance Midrash

For young beginners, go back to the same exercise found in the "Motivating Movement" section, except add the idea of five work movements, one transition movement, and a rest. Repeat the pattern until the group has established it well and has enjoyed moving in the pattern.

For more advanced groups: Each person is to establish his/her own tempo and develop a phrase of seven equal parts. (For those who know music, each part can equal a measure in the timing they choose to work in.) The first five parts are to be in an active, busy style, the sixth part is a transition to the seventh, which depicts the dancers' interpretation of the phrase "ceased all work." The seventh part may be a total stop or a restful, sustained movement. Divide the group in half so that the dancers can watch each other. Coach individuals to go with their own rhythm. Some will be doing active movements, while others are resting. Point out how this relates to various degrees of Shabbat observance.

Challenge

God created male and female on the sixth day. Create a dance which portrays what the first male and female might have been doing on the seventh day, the first Shabbat. Some possibilities are:

A playful dance of discovering how they can move and what is around them.

A quiet acknowledging of themselves and what is immediately around them. (Time and great care should be taken as each movement is made.)

A blessing by them of the day. (Since they are created in God's image, they intuitively understand to bless the day as God does.)

Genesis
Beginner ■ □ □

Naming the Creatures

> And God formed out of the earth all the wild beasts and all the birds of the sky, and brought them to the man to see what he would call them; and whatever the man called each living creature that would be its name. (Genesis 2:19)

Description

This is part of the second version of the creation story. In Genesis 1, God created animals before Adam; however, in Genesis 2, God created animals after Adam and Adam gave them their names.

Motivating Movement

Note: This motivating movement section can be used as a way to get to know everyone's name.

1. Have the group sit in a circle. Go around the circle having each person clap his/her name.
2. Have everyone get up and dance the rhythm of their names, repeating their names several times.
3. Progress to everyone singing and dancing their names with movement, conveying something important about themselves. Their dance might emphasize one of their physical characteristics such as being tall, or portray one of their favorite hobbies, such as horseback riding.

Dance Midrash

One person is chosen to be Adam. Everyone else is to be a mythical creature. Begin by having the group spend time improvising the mythical creatures. When they have the creatures' characteristics well defined, each person can present his/her creature to Adam to be named while the others watch. Adam may need to dance with the creature, inspect it, and even ask it questions in order to determine its name.

Making Connections

Everyone is to share what they know about their given names. Were they named after someone? How have their names affected them? If they don't like their names, what other names might they want?

Challenge

Have the group improvise a dance about Adam and Eve. Base the dance on the names Adam and Eve.

See Genesis 2:7 ("God formed man from the dust of the earth. God blew into his nostrils the breath of life and man became a living being"). The Hebrew word for man, Adam, is related to *adamah*, the word for earth and to *dam*, the word for blood.

In Genesis 3:20, "The man named his wife Eve, because she was the mother of all the living." The name Eve in Hebrew is *Chavah* and it comes from the word *chai*, which means living.

Genesis
Advanced ■ ■ ■

Discovery

They perceived that they were naked. (Genesis 3:7)

Description

The woman, encouraged by the serpent, ate from the tree in the middle of the garden. God had warned her not to eat from this tree. She offered the fruit to her husband, who also ate it. As God had warned, their eyes "were opened." The first thing they discovered was that they were naked.

Motivating Movement

1. Have dancers imagine they are in high heels or business shoes, a tight skirt or suit, stockings, girdle, tie, long sleeves. They are to dance as if wearing these clothes. Have them gradually pretend to take the clothes off until they have nothing on and can move as freely as they like.

Making Connections

Every child enjoys a time of innocence, marked by a certain freedom and lack of inhibition. As we grow up, we become self-conscious of ourselves and our bodies. Lead a discussion about the transition time when we first began to feel awkward and aware of our bodies. How did this awareness affect the way we acted, moved, and talked?

Dance Midrash

Have the participants begin by moving freely, without being self-conscious, enjoying themselves. Each person finds his/her own moment (symbolic of the moment when the man and the woman perceived they were naked), and expresses that moment in dance. Concentrate first on perceiving one's own nakedness and then progress to discovering the nakedness of others in the group.

Challenge

In Genesis 3:10 the man says, "I was afraid because I was naked." The perception of his nakedness led to fear. Improvise on the word naked from a physical point of view, as well as from a religious or spiritual point of view, i.e., with the appropriate accompanying emotions. Ask the dancers to remember a time when they felt particularly vulnerable or exposed and to add this feeling to the improvisation. In Genesis 3:10 the man's fear is a result of realizing his nakedness or vulnerability, not the fact he has done something wrong. Coach participants to show this vulnerability.

Genesis
Beginner ■ □ □

Bursting of the Floodgates

> All the fountains of the great deep burst apart, and the floodgates of the sky broke open. The rain fell on the earth forty days and forty nights. (Genesis 7:11–12)

Description

Noah, described as the only righteous man in his generation, followed God's instructions and built an ark. As Noah was commanded, he gathered together his family, two pairs of every animal and bird, and brought them into the ark. It began to rain, and the rain continued for forty days and nights.

Motivating Movement

1. Talk about the sound that raindrops make when they hit the window or pavement. Ask dancers to put that sound into their feet and practice short staccato jumping, prancing, and hopping movements. Now put the staccato movement in other parts of the body, such as hands, elbows, and shoulders. When the staccato movement is clearly understood and experienced, expand to percussive movement, portraying the words "burst apart" and "broke open." Finally have the group improvise starting with percussive "bursting apart" movement and leading into continuous staccato movement.

2. Have dancers imagine that they are animals in a crowded limited space, for example, an elephant in a circus railroad car. A good way to introduce this is to bring in pictures of animals and birds, a different animal or bird on each card. Ask participants to select a card. The animal on the card is the one they portray in the improvisation.

Dance Midrash

Divide the group in half. One half portrays the animals inside of the ark, while the other half is the rain. Remember to define the space of the ark and remind the "animals" that they will have to confine their movement to that space. The rain group can move in the remaining space surrounding the ark. Coach the rain group to be continuous in maintaining the staccato movement. Keep the improvisation going until the feeling of impatience in the animals is well established.

Making Connections

Ask dancers: "What are your feelings when the weather has been bad and you are forced to stay indoors? How do you react when the bad weather continues for several days in a row? If you felt impatient, how did you express this feeling?" Ask how Noah and his family might have felt being cooped up in the ark. Ask how they might have felt when they realized that they were the only people God saved.

Challenge

1. Have the group portray some natural phenomena which result in disasters or loss of life. For example, the group might portray the hot sun parching the ground causing crops to die and famine to occur, or lava of a volcano pouring down a mountain and wiping out a community. After dancing, consider discussing such natural events—why do they happen, what purpose do they serve?
2. Have the group develop a Dance Midrash about the character of Noah during the 40 days and nights of rain. What are the different emotions he might have felt as the rain continued? Possibilities include:
    Thankfulness that he and his family were given the chance to begin again
    Impatience as a result of being in the ark for so many days
    Fear and doubt
    Desire to take care of his family, the animals, and birds

Genesis
Beginner ■ □ □

Gibberish

That is why it was called Babel, because there God confounded the speech of the whole earth; and from there God scattered them over the face of the whole earth. (Genesis 11:9)

Description

Since everyone on earth spoke the same language, it was easy for them to work together. In the valley of Shinar, the people built a city and a tower with its top in the sky. God, seeing what they had done, mixed up their speech so that they could not understand each other. They stopped building and were scattered from their central location.

Motivating Movement

1. Bring in pictures of unique architecture, especially tall buildings. Divide participants into small groups of 3 to 5 dancers. Each group is to create the illusion of one of the tall buildings through the shapes they make together. They might want to use chairs to give more height to their design. Have them share their designs with each other.
2. Divide the group into pairs. Ask the pairs to find movement which requires cooperation from both of them to accomplish it. In particular, stress movements in which they share their body weights in some way.

3. Have the group practice speaking gibberish, vocal utterances which are not recognizable words. Coach the group to keep normal speech rhythm while avoiding real words. When the group is used to speaking in gibberish, ask them to accompany it with movement. (The use of gibberish in improvisational work was developed by Viola Spolin and is described in *Theatre Game File*, published by Cemreal, Inc., St. Louis, Missouri, 1975.)

Dance Midrash

Have the group establish very cooperative building movements representative of building the city and tower. Encourage them to stress that they are dedicated to accomplishing their goal. When the leader feels they have established a mood of dedication, call out the word "gibberish." The group then begins speaking only in gibberish; they do not understand each other. They no longer want to work together and are in a state of total confusion.

Making Connections

Ask the group to address the question of why God was displeased with the building of the city and tower and decided to put an end to it. The only reason given in Torah is: "This is how they have begun to act" (see Genesis 11:6). Share the following Midrash with the group:

> As the tower became taller, it took over a year to get bricks from the base to the upper stories. . . . If a brick slipped and fell, the people cried, but when a man fell and died, no one seemed to care.

Ask for examples of the same kind of reaction toward events today.

Challenge

First, because the earth had become corrupt and lawless, God caused a flood to destroy all but Noah, his family, and the animals. Then God found dissatisfaction in the building of the city. Divide the group in half. One half is to improvise the corruption and lawlessness that existed before the flood, and the other group improvises the society at the time of the building of the city and tower of Babel ("this is how they have begun to act"). Have them watch each other, switch parts, and dance again. Discuss the similarities and differences between the two situations.

Genesis
Intermediate ■ ■ ☐

Abram, Go Forth

> God said to Abram, "Go forth from your native land and from your father's house to the land that I will show you."
> (Genesis 12:1)

Description

This is the first time God spoke to Abram. God told Abram to go forth, to leave his homeland and his father's house. God continued by letting Abram know that he will be a great nation and be blessed.

Motivating Movement

1. Have the group practice bold movement patterns which go across the room. Some examples are:
    4 bold walks, 2 skips
    Run, run, leap
    Step skip, step leap
    Continuous big, low walks
   Teach the specific patterns first and then have the group invent their own.
2. Have the group improvise outgoing, expansive movement.

Making Connections

Lead a discussion during which participants share examples of times they "went forth," such as the first day of kindergarten, going away to overnight camp, or getting a first apartment. What different emotions and reactions did they have at such times?

Dance Midrash

Everyone is Abram at the moment when Abram follows God's instructions to "go forth." The improvisation is to explore the different emotions Abram feels as he goes from his homeland and his parents' house. Some possibilities are:

Reluctance to leave the familiar

Excitement about the unknown

Observant of everything around him as he begins his new journey

A sense of being alone and a stranger in the new place to which he is going

Inner strength as a result of being chosen by God

Challenge

In the Torah God talks and appears to the leaders of the Israelites in different ways. Have each person choose one of the leaders. Ask them to review the scene when God first appears to the leader and to analyze the unique elements of the scene. They then are to develop a solo dance of the character's first dialogue with God. Three suggested scenes are:

Noah getting specific instructions from God about the flood, the building of the ark, and all that he is to do (see Genesis 6:13–21)

Abram being told to go forth and that he will found a nation (see Genesis 12:1–3)

Moses seeing God for the first time. Moses revealing his fears and reluctance to assume a leadership role, and God encouraging him to take on the leadership role (see Exodus 3:1–4:17)

Genesis
Intermediate ■ ■ □

Sister . . . Let Me Live!

> *Please say that you are my sister, that it may go well with me because of you, and that I may remain alive thanks to you.*
> (Genesis 12:13)

Description

There was a famine in the land, causing Abram and Sarai to go to Egypt where food was more plentiful. As Abram was about to enter Egypt, he said to his wife Sarai, "I know what a beautiful woman you are. If the Egyptians see you and think, 'She is his wife,' they will kill me and let you live." Sarai played the role of Abram's sister and was taken into Pharaoh's court. Pharaoh eventually found out Sarai's identity and sent Abram and Sarai away, along with the possessions that Abram had acquired during the sojourn.

Motivating Movement

1. Have dancers improvise playful movement. Ask them gradually to introduce into the "playfulness" a sense of flirtation and romance.
2. Have each dancer imagine a stationary person somewhere in the space. The dancer is to "interact" with the imaginary person, going from loyalty to desertion and back again to loyalty.

Making Connections

This verse inspires reflection on how sibling and spousal relationships are and are not interrelated. Ask dancers to describe the ideal relationship with a sibling. Next, ask them to list qualities they feel are most important to find in a mate. Where do the values concerning both types of relationships overlap? In what ways would they want to seek a lifetime partner who reflects aspects of the ideal sibling relationship?

Dance Midrash

Divide the group into pairs. One person is Abram, the other is Sarai. Have the pairs imagine the dialogue that would have followed Abram's request that Sarai pose as his sister. Examples are:

Sarai is confused and asks Abram to explain further.

Sarai foresees what will happen, yet cannot think of an alternative.

Sarai resists Abram's suggestion. Although Abram finally convinces her to go along with his request, she is resentful.

Challenge

One way of understanding the complicated dynamic of the marriage bond is to recognize the various roles spouses play in each other's lives. Some of the roles may be: best friend, lover, sibling, child, parent, business partner.

Divide the group into pairs and have them improvise on the marriage relationship. Explore different spousal roles which are continually in flux. Have them pay close attention to how they must adjust their movement based on how their partner is moving. For example, what happens when both partners "play" the child in need of parenting or when both "play" the parent who wants to take charge?

The leader may find it helpful to encourage movement to happen spontaneously, with dancers reacting to and initiating movement without pre-planning and over-intellectualizing.

Genesis
Intermediate ■ ■ □

Sarah Laughed

And Sarah laughed. (Genesis 18:12)

Description

Sarah and Abraham provided hospitality to three messengers. The messengers, possibly angels sent by God, told Sarah that she would become pregnant and have the child that she and Abraham wanted. Sarah, ninety years old, had given up all hope of having a child. When she heard the news, she laughed.

Motivating Movement

1. Have dancers begin by putting the rhythm and gesture of laughter in their shoulders, then in their feet, then in their legs. Have them continue putting the laughter in different parts of their bodies until the laughter is expanded throughout their whole bodies. Have them make laughing turns and laughing jumps.
2. Ask dancers to walk as if they are ninety years old and to make arm gestures as a ninety-year-old would. Have them improvise a dance as if they were ninety years old hearing joyful news.

Making Connections

Ask the group: "What was your reaction when you were the recipient of real or imagined wonderful news (got a good grade, won the lottery, a medical test came back negative, a marriage announcement, job promotion)?" Ask them to relive the scenario, seeing themselves laughing as they hear the news. Encourage them to take this emotion into the Dance Midrash.

Dance Midrash

Everyone in the group is Sarah who has just heard that she will have a child. Each is to improvise a dance based on laughing, keeping in mind that Sarah was ninety years old. The different emotions behind their laughter are important to this improvisation and might include joy, confusion and shock, disbelief, fear, mocking, and fulfillment. Follow the improvisation with discussion and repeat with expanded suggestions from the group.

Challenge

Sarah and Abraham name their son Isaac. Isaac comes from the word "laughter" in Hebrew. Have the dancers develop solos portraying either Sarah or Abraham. Begin with laughing after hearing the news and end with the naming of Isaac. (See Genesis 18:9–15 and 21:1–8.)

Genesis
Beginner ■ □ □

Lot's Wife

Lot's wife looked back and thereupon turned into a pillar of salt.
(Genesis 19:26)

Description

God was about to destroy the cities of Sodom and Gomorrah. Lot's family, the only righteous people, having been extremely hospitable to two messengers, were to be saved. The messengers told Lot to take his wife and his two unwed daughters and leave the city. Lot was hesitant to leave. The two messengers took the family by the hand and ran with them saying, "Flee for your life! Do not look behind you." As they fled, Sodom and Gomorrah were destroyed by fire. Lot's wife looked back.

Motivating Movement

1. Have dancers, one at a time, do the following pattern: Run, stop, turn around, and freeze into a unique shape. (Repeat several times.)
2. Have dancers practice sustained movement.
3. Ask dancers to be a tear slowly falling down a cheek.

Dance Midrash

Everyone turns into a pillar of salt as Lot's wife did. Salt formations can be affected by wind and rain, gradually changing shape over long periods of time. The dancers are to be changed slowly by the wind and rain so that they very gradually intensify the reaction Lot's wife might have felt as she looked back and was transformed. Some possible reactions are:

Grief
Compassion
Horror
Fear

Making Connections

Share experiences and feelings about moving away and, in particular, how it felt to leave a neighborhood or your house for the final time. Ask the group: "Did you want to take one last look?"

Challenge

The Torah tells us nothing about Lot's wife except that she looked back. In fact, her name is not even given. The following modern Midrash beautifully describes Lot's wife, giving her a name and developing details about her personality, actions, and reactions.

> When the Angels of God came that morning to urge Lot, Tova, and their two daughters to hurry to leave Sodom before it was too late, Tova was already at work gathering their belongings. She knew that her home and the homes of all of her friends were going to be destroyed. Tova pushed these thoughts from her mind. They were too painful. She must not think of what was coming. She must just get everything ready. "Let's see," she thought to herself, "we will need blankets, water jugs, oil, spices, flour...." The list seemed endless. She sent her daughters to the kitchen to get the necessary food and utensils while she went from room to room collecting the things of value that could be carried.
>
> Reprinted with permission from *Taking the Fruit: Modern Women's Midrash on the Bible* (San Diego: Women's Institute for Continuing Jewish Education, 1989), 37.

The group may do one of the following:
Create a dance using the details in this modern midrash.
Create their own set of details and dance them.

Genesis
Intermediate ■ ■ ☐

Hagar's Eyes Are Opened

> *Then God opened her eyes and she saw a well of water. She went and filled the skin with water and let the boy drink.* (Genesis 21:19)

Description

Sarah, barren for many years, gave her handmaid Hagar to Abraham so that he might have an offspring. Hagar bore Ishmael. Years after, Sarah finally (at 90) gave birth to Isaac. Sarah, uncertain of how Ishmael was relating to her son Isaac, told Abraham to send away Hagar and her son. In the wilderness Hagar and Ishmael ran out of the short supply of water Abraham had sent with them. Hagar was desperate. Ready to give up, but not wanting to watch her child die, she sat down a short distance from him and burst into tears.

Motivating Movement

1. Beginning on one side of the space, have dancers move across it as if they are fleeing. Repeat, slowing the pace, but maintaining the intensity and desperation of fleeing. On the last repetition, have dancers move very slowly, with their eyes closed. (Assign some participants to spot the dancers whose eyes are closed.)

2. Have dancers lie comfortably on the floor. "Paint" an image similar to this: "Imagine your hands are covered with dozens of closed eyes. . . . Your arms are covered with many, many closed eyes. . . ." Continue going slowly through all the body parts. When the whole body is "covered," tell participants to open their eyes, all of the "eyes," and begin to move with a new sense of openness and awareness.

Making Connections

Ask participants to think of a time when they haven't been able to see what was obvious. Examples are: not being able to find their keys, then finally realizing the keys were in their hand all along; or not seeing the traffic light turn green until cars behind them started honking. What made them finally see?

Taking it a step further, when haven't they been able to see what in retrospect was obvious because of a blind spot in their self-perception? Was the blind spot stubbornness, jealousy, greed, competitiveness? What made them finally see?

Dance Midrash

Participants are to dance the role of Hagar at different stages: as she is sent into the wilderness, as she wanders with her son, as she becomes more and more desperate, and as she is about to give up. Have them keep in mind the idea of being "closed," unaware. At the moment when Hagar finally gives up, she is forced to open her eyes ("God opened her eyes"). Dancers focus on how to respond to a God who pushes them to "see."

Challenge

Why was it that Hagar didn't see the well? Have dancers throw out possibilities such as:

> She was so worried about her son Ishmael that her eyes were focused on him and not on the land around her.
> Being exhausted and thirsty, she wasn't able to lift her eyes to see.
> She didn't see the well because there was no well. God opened Hagar's eyes and simultaneously made a well to appear.

Each dancer chooses the possibility he/she wishes to express in the improvisation and dances in ways that suggest the emotions or reasons behind Hagar not seeing.

Genesis
Intermediate ■ ■ □

The Binding of Isaac

> And he said *"Here I am."* (Genesis 22:1)
> And he said *"Here I am."* (Genesis 22:7)
> And he said *"Here I am."* (Genesis 22:11)

Description

God called to Abraham to test his faith. Abraham, ready to follow God's instruction to take his son Isaac to Mt. Moriah and sacrifice him, said, "Here I am." As Abraham and Isaac approached the site, Isaac called to his father, and Abraham said, "Here I am." The third time Abraham answered, "Here I am," he was about to carry out God's instructions to slay Isaac.

Motivating Movement

1. Have dancers stand in a circle. One at a time, in either English or Hebrew, have dancers say, "Here I am" or *"Hineni"* while at the same time making a movement which expresses the person's mood at that moment. The group repeats the movement. Continue until everyone in the circle has had a turn.
2. Stand in a circle and continue developing movement from the phrase "Here I am." Point out that the rhythm of the phrase is three equal counts. One person begins by creating a three count phrase expressing "Here I

am." The next person repeats the first person's phrase and then adds on another phrase of his/her own. Continue the pattern, seeing how many phrases can be remembered and how many different movement phrases can demonstrate "Here I am." When the phrase becomes too long for the group to remember, start a new one.

Dance Midrash

Everyone in the group is Abraham. First, have everyone create movement which expresses Abraham the first time he says, "Here I am." Second, continue by expressing the emotion that Abraham feels as he answers "Here I am" to his son on their way up Mt. Moriah. Third, explore the moment when Abraham has the knife in his hand and is about to slay Isaac and again says, "Here I am." The final step is for each person to improvise going back and forth, at his/her own pace, between the three moments.

Making Connections

Talk about the fact that while Abraham is the main actor in the scene, a lot of other people are affected by his actions. Ask the group how Sarah and Isaac might have been affected. Ask the group to share examples from their own lives in which one person's actions dramatically affected the lives of the people around them. Some examples are:

Head of household takes a job in a new community.

A member of a family commits suicide.

A member of a class steals money from the teacher's drawer.

Challenge

Ask each person to choose a character other than Abraham who is connected to the events in the story. Each person is to create a dance that reflects how that character might say "Here I am" at the critical moment in the story when Abraham is about to slay Isaac. Some examples are:

Isaac: Is he a willing sacrifice or is he struggling to get free?

Sarah: Does she know what is happening or is she (ironically) doing routine tasks? If she knows, how might she be acting? Praying for God to stop the test? Grief stricken?

The ram: Moving freely about, not aware that he will soon be sacrificed

The angel: Ready to be the messenger if God decides to stop the action

Genesis
Intermediate ■ ■ □

Sarah's Lifetime

Sarah's lifetime—the span of Sarah's life—came to one hundred and twenty seven years. (Genesis 23:1)

Description

Sarah died. No cause of her death was given. Abraham negotiated with the Hittites for her burial site.

Motivating Movement

1. Have the group explore movement representative of the different stages of life.
   a. Prenatal movement, the floating type of movement experienced before birth
   b. The early movements of the baby, such as reaching for an object, lifting the head and rolling over
   c. The toddler learning to walk, and then once that is mastered, eagerly exploring
   d. The free exuberant movement of childhood
   e. The "cool" style of moving in the teen years
   f. The responsible, controlled moving of adults

g. The movement of elderly people, walking perhaps with a cane and posture not quite erect

Making Connections

Ask the group to remember being with someone who is either very old and near death or very sick, knowing he/she will die. Often the sick or dying person is eager to remember important times in his/her life. Have the group share such experiences and their reactions to them.

Dance Midrash

As Sarah is about to die, images from important moments in her life flash through her mind. Have dancers be these fleeting images that flash through her memory. Some possibilities are:
    Abraham telling Sarah how beautiful she is and the danger her beauty caused them
    Sarah's jealousy of Hagar
    Sarah's frustration at not bearing a child until her old age
    Sarah's joy in Isaac's birth
    Sarah's bewilderment when Abraham takes Isaac on the journey to Moriah

Challenge

1. According to a midrash, Sarah died because Abraham returned alone from Moriah. Sarah, believing that Isaac had been sacrificed, died of grief. Sarah is never mentioned during the telling of the *Akedah* (binding of Isaac). Have the group imagine that God spoke not only to Abraham, but to Sarah as well. Both of them are instructed to take their son and sacrifice him. Think of Sarah's different choices and the actions she might have taken, such as going with Abraham to Moriah, arguing against God's instructions, or staying at home overwhelmed by the instructions and pretending she never heard them.
    Divide the group into trios. Have the trios outline a dance of Abraham, Sarah, and Isaac, portraying a new telling of the *Akedah* in which Sarah's actions and reactions play an important part. The trio is to conclude with Sarah's death. Have the trios practice their ideas in dance and then share them with each other.

2. Have the group portray Abraham giving a eulogy which recalls the role Sarah played in his life. Read Genesis 23:2–20 to get a sense of Abraham's actions after Sarah's death and the importance he placed on obtaining a burial site. The eulogy might be expanded to include rituals he might have performed while burying Sarah in the cave he bought.

Genesis
Advanced ■ ■ ■

Rebekah's Veil

So she took her veil and covered herself. (Genesis 24:65)

Description

Abraham sent his trusted servant to find a bride for Isaac. The servant returned with Rebekah. Isaac was out walking in the field and saw the camels approaching. Rebekah, seeing a man walking in the field, asked who he was. When she learned it was Isaac, her husband to be, she took her veil and covered herself.

Motivating Movement

1. Bring in several 2'-3' squares of lightweight fabric (ideally a piece of fabric for each person in the group). Ask the participants to move with the fabric, playing freely with it. If there are not enough pieces to go around, have pairs or trios share the fabric. Next, coach the group to experiment with the fabric by putting it on or covering parts of their bodies with it, particularly their faces. Have them move with the fabric as they wear it or cover their faces with it.

Making Connections

Lead a discussion on how we use clothes and accessories to reflect moods we want to convey at particular times. Ask individuals to be specific as they describe the mood they felt as they wore a particular garment. Ask them to create a dance imagining they are wearing the particular garment. Coach them to reveal the mood they described.

Dance Midrash

Ask the female dancers in the group to be Rebekah at the moment she knows that the man in the field is Isaac. Use the pieces of fabric as props in the improvisation and encourage the dancers to demonstrate the different feelings Rebekah might have had, such as shyness, modesty, fear, and/or pride.

Have the male dancers portray Isaac realizing that the woman he sees is his bride to be. Use the pieces of fabric as props, perhaps as shepherds' blankets. Would he react by reaching out to her, shyly hiding, nervously waiting, and/or becoming playful?

Discuss the similarities and differences between the reactions of Isaac and Rebekah. If the Dance Midrash is repeated, duets can portray Isaac and Rebekah at their first meeting.

Challenge

Two other passages in Genesis refer to veils. Leah, covered with a veil, pretended to be Rachel and was married to Jacob (Genesis 29:22–23). In that instance, the veil was used to conceal an identity. In the story of Tamar (Genesis 38:1–19), Tamar covered herself with a veil in order to look different. Her husband, Judah's son, had died and she was sent back to her father's house. When she heard Judah was coming, she took off her widow's garb, covered her face with a veil, and wrapped herself in it. Judah saw her and thought she was a harlot.

Have the group use the fabric and explore in dance Rebekah, Leah, and Tamar. Transitions from one character to another should be reflected in the way the veil is used and in the emotions conveyed.

Genesis
Intermediate ■ ■ □

Jacob Emerges

Then his brother emerged, holding on to the heel of Esau, so they named him Jacob. (Genesis 25:26)

Description

Rebekah, Isaac's wife, was pregnant with twins who struggled within her. God told Rebekah that the older son would serve the younger. Esau was born first and Jacob followed immediately, holding on to his older brother's heel. (The name Jacob is actually a play on the Hebrew word *akev*—heel.)

Motivating Movement

1. Have the group practice reaching movements. See how many different ways they can reach. Coach them to reach from different positions, such as sitting, lying on their stomachs, lying on their backs, kneeling, and standing.
2. Have them practice aggressive reaching with the purpose of not letting anyone get ahead of them.
3. Have them practice holding on to an imaginary partner with the intent of stopping or slowing the partner.

Making Connections

Ask dancers to draw from their life experiences, improvising on a recent time when they felt particularly competitive with a sibling or with a friend. While they are dancing, encourage them not to pantomime the incident, but to dance their feelings.

Dance Midrash

Have everyone in the group dance the role of Jacob wanting to be "first." Have them use the reaching and holding movements and the competitive feelings practiced earlier. The dancers are to limit space by drawing imaginary circles no more than 3' in diameter around themselves. They are not to move out of the space. However, they can move as strongly and as aggressively as they like. (Percussive accompaniment works very well for this improvisation.)

Challenge

For advanced and older dancers, especially trained dancers who have worked often with each other, work in pairs exploring competitive movement. Encourage lifts and partner work.

Genesis
Intermediate ■ ■ □

Jacob: One Who Disguises

> Jacob said to his father, "I am Esau, your firstborn; I have done as you told me. Pray sit up and eat of my game, that you may give me your innermost blessing." (Genesis 27:19)

Description

Isaac was to give his "innermost blessing" to his eldest son Esau. However, Rebekah wanted this special blessing to go to their younger son Jacob. She disguised Jacob in Esau's clothing and covered Jacob's neck with the skins of young goats. Jacob went to his blind father and received the blessing intended for Esau. Isaac's blessing was: "May God give you of the dew of heaven and the fat of the earth, abundance of new grain and wine. Let peoples serve you, and nations bow to you; be master over your brothers, and let your mother's sons bow to you. Cursed be they who curse you, blessed be they who bless you" (Genesis 27:28–29).

Motivating Movement

1. Have the dancers improvise moving with a cape, fake fur coat, or heavy blanket. Coach them to explore different ways they can dance with the "cloak" as they wear it in various ways.

2. Have the group improvise on the theme of discomfort. Coach them to explore movement that reflects both physical discomfort and emotional or spiritual discomfort.

Dance Midrash

Real or imagined capes, fake fur coats, or heavy blankets are needed for this improvisation. All dancers are Jacob. There are three parts to this improvisation.

Jacob dances as himself: Dancers begin by moving in ways they think reflect the personality of Jacob. Remind them that Jacob is described as being a "mild man, who stayed in camp" (Genesis 25:27).

Jacob disguises as Esau: When Jacob's personality has been fully expressed in movement, dancers continue by moving with their real or imaginary "cloaks." They dance with the cloaks as if the cloaks are what transform Jacob into his disguise as Esau, "a skillful hunter, a man of the outdoors" (Genesis 25:27). Coach dancers to be sensitive to feelings Jacob must have experienced as he prepared to deceive his father (with the urging of his mother).

Jacob comes into his father's presence: Dancers end by imagining that they come before Isaac and request his "innermost blessing."

Making Connections

Ask the group for reasons people might hide their personal identity, religion, or nationality.

Jacob is one among many in Jewish history who disguise themselves. For example, Tamar disguised as a harlot, Joseph disguised himself before his brothers, and Esther concealed her identity as a Jew. Esther didn't hide her personal identity, but she did "disguise" her religious identity. Other Jews also have hidden their Jewish identity in order to save their own or others' lives—Marranos practiced Judaism secretly during the Inquisition, and many European Jews tried to "disguise" their Jewish ancestry in order to elude the Nazis.

Even now, in places where Jews are free, some try to disguise their Jewish heritage. Lead a discussion on what some of the reasons for this might be. Possibilities include: fear of being different, concern about anti-Semitism, confusion about God, close friends not being Jewish, desire to participate in "mainstream" religious celebrations (i.e., Christmas), etc.

Challenge

Refer to the section "Making Connections" above. This challenge may be especially appropriate for Purim. Have dancers create solos in which they explore and try to resolve through dance a situation of discomfort concerning Jewish identity. They may choose to be someone in the past, such as Esther, or someone in the present day. Coach them to express the reasons behind the discomfort. (Reasons might range from real danger to concern about achieving fame with a Jewish sounding name.)

Genesis
Beginner ■ □ □

Jacob's Dream

He had a dream; a stairway was set on the ground and its top reached to the sky, and angels of God were going up and down on it. (Genesis 28:12)

Description

Jacob, in fleeing from his brother Esau, came to a place and laid down to sleep. He dreamed of a ladder with angels going up and coming down. God told him that he and his offspring would inherit the land on which he was lying, and that his descendants would spread out in all directions.

Motivating Movement

1. With young children, use a stairway. Have an older group imagine a stairway. The dancers practice going up and down the stairs in a variety of ways—boldly, gracefully, mysteriously, separately or attached to others.
2. Have dancers experiment with movement that is grounded and earthy, and movement that reaches the sky. Coach them to contrast the two types of movement as much as possible.

Making Connections

Ask the group to share what they believe to be true about angels. For example, are angels agents of God, projections of our best selves, images of loved ones in other guises, forces of emotions, mystical energies, etc.? How might angels be experienced in our lives today?

Dance Midrash

Divide dancers into groups of four. Three of the dancers are angels and one is Jacob. Jacob starts by lying down. The three "angels," after clarifying what exactly they represent, dance as if they are reflecting Jacob's dream. After Jacob witnesses the angels' dance, he can leave his sleeping body, dance a response to the angels, and return to his sleeping position.

Challenge

Jacob's dream about the angels was not necessarily the only dream he had that night. Ask the group to consider that the dream about the angels was the culmination of several dreams leading up to it. In the improvisation, the group dances what may have been the three or four dreams preceding that in the text. They should dance these dreams in a way that leads them to conclude with the dream in the verse. Direct the group to pay attention to transitions between dreams—that is, there should be some thread that connects one dream to the next.

Genesis
Beginner ■ □ □

Jacob's Journey Continues

Jacob lifted his feet. (Genesis 29:1)

Description

Jacob was on his way to Haran. After his dream he named the site Bethel, house of God. He resumed his journey ("lifted his feet") and came to the land of the Easterners. Shortly after his arrival, he met Rachel.

Motivating Movement

1. Have dancers walk across the space:
   a. Normally
   b. As if they are chasing their feet
   c. As if their feet are chasing the rest of their bodies

Dance Midrash

Usually people are carried along by their feet, but here Jacob lifts or carries his feet. Two midrashic explanations contradict one another. One says he was reluctant to leave the place where he experienced such a powerful vision and therefore he had to carry his feet (drag himself) out of Bethel. The other view is that as a result of the Divine promise, he became light-footed with joy and eagerly rushed forward to begin a new life.

Designate part of the room to be the sacred place Jacob named Bethel. Each dancer is Jacob and begins moving in the sacred space. When he is ready to leave and resume his journey, he "lifts his feet." The way the dancers move from the sacred space should reflect their understanding of the words "Jacob lifted his feet"—reluctance or light-footed joy.

Making Connections

Have the participants share their feelings about a place that is special to them (camp, grandparents' home, a cabin in the woods or on a beach, etc.). Ask how they feel when they leave that place—are they reluctant, or do they rush out without looking back?

Challenge

Jacob didn't know it, but perhaps he was lifting his feet with lightness and joy because he was soon to meet his future love, Rachel. Ask the dancers to choreograph his dance of joy. No reason should be given for the joy; the goal is rather to create movement that is celebratory and joyful in itself.

Genesis
Intermediate ■ ■ □

Sisters: Leah and Rachel

Leah had weak eyes; Rachel was shapely and beautiful. (Genesis 29:17)

Description

Rachel and Leah were the two daughters of Laban. Leah, the older one, had weak eyes, while Rachel, the younger, was beautiful. Jacob, having seen Rachel at the well and fallen in love with her, wanted to marry her in exchange for work he did for Laban.

Motivating Movement

1. Have dancers experiment with improvising phrases of movement that emphasize dynamic changes. Some examples are:
    a. Moving slowly, then quickly, then as fast as possible, and ending by stopping abruptly
    b. Moving in a fast staccato manner, then in a slow, strong, percussive way
    c. Beginning by making small jumps and gradually increasing the jumps until they are bigger
    d. Turning quickly and then slowly, ending with a fall to the ground

Dance Midrash

Divide the group into the following four parts:
- Sitting on the far right: This group will whisper "Rachel was shapely and beautiful" (in either English or Hebrew).
- Sitting on the far left: This group will whisper "Leah had weak eyes" (in either English or Hebrew).
- Standing in the middle of the room: This group will portray Rachel.
- Standing in the middle of the room: This group will portray Leah.

The two groups portraying Rachel and Leah begin by moving as young, playful, and innocent girls. When they have clearly established this mood, the sitting groups begin whispering their lines. The dancers portraying Rachel and Leah respond to what they are hearing. Rachel's movements take on the qualities of shapely and beautiful, while Leah's movements portray weak eyes or the effect of having weak eyes. As the whispers continue and increase in intensity, the dynamic level of the movement qualities also increase. When there is a clear difference in movement styles and the dynamics have reached a high intensity, end the improvisation. Change parts and continue until everyone has had an opportunity to do all four parts.

Making Connections

Ask everyone to think about what single word or phrase their parents would use to describe them or their siblings. Ask what this labeling does to them. Do they tend to follow it and reinforce the description, or rebel against it to disprove it?

Challenge

Building from the discussion in "Making Connections" above, have each person dance his/her "label" and his/her reaction to it. (For example, the older and smart one, the baby of the family, etc.)

Expand by having those who wish to do so direct a scene in which other members of the group portray his/her family, dancing the various family members' "labels."

Genesis
Intermediate ■ ■ □

Jacob Wrestles

Jacob was left alone. And a man wrestled with him until the break of dawn.
(Genesis 32:25)

Description

Twenty years earlier Jacob had received his father's blessing and fled, afraid of Esau's revenge. Now, it was the night before Jacob's reunion with his brother Esau. Separating himself from his wives and children, Jacob prepared for the reunion. Alone, he wrestled with a man.

Motivating Movement

1. Explore movement related to sports activities, such as:
    a. Baseball: reaching to catch a fly ball or sliding into home plate
    b. Basketball: dribbling the ball or shooting a basket using a jump or leap
2. Have each person imagine that he/she is a wrestler practicing wrestling holds on an imaginary person. Do this in a slow, sustained manner.
    Next have each person imagine he/she is the one being held in the various holds. Slowly move from one held position to another. Do this in a slow, sustained manner.

Dance Midrash

Divide the group into three sections. Each section will portray an interpretation of the identity of Jacob's wrestling partner. Three possible interpretations are:

Jacob himself

Esau

an angel

One section at a time improvises Jacob's wrestling based on an assigned interpretation. After all the sections have shared their improvisations, discuss how the movements of the three sections differed.

Making Connections

Ask each person to remember a time of preparing for a reunion with a close friend or family member with whom tensions had existed. Discuss the feelings each person had at the time and how he/she dealt with them.

Ask if anyone experienced restless nights or dreamed about the person prior to the reunion. Point out that their experiences may have been similar to Jacob's.

Challenge

1. Jacob was left with a permanent physical reminder following his dream, a strained thigh which caused him to limp. His name was also changed to Israel—one who wrestles with God. Have each dancer choose one of the interpretations from the Dance Midrash. Add a beginning and ending to the improvisation which illustrates that Jacob is changed by his encounter.
2. In an earlier dream, Jacob envisioned angels going up and down a ladder (see Genesis 28:12). Using the interpretation that Jacob was wrestling with an angel, have the dancers improvise being the angel who appeared and reappeared to Jacob. Coach them to give the angel a definite ongoing role in Jacob's life. For example, the angel might encourage Jacob's awakening to new spiritual awareness at critical times in his life and represent this awakening energy.

Genesis
Advanced ■ ■ ■

Dinah

Now Dinah, the daughter whom Leah had born to Jacob, went out to visit the daughters of the land. (Genesis 34:1)

Description

Dinah was the only daughter of Jacob. When Dinah went out to join the other women of the land, she was taken by Shechem, a Hivite, who lay with her by force. Shechem spoke tenderly to her and wanted to marry her. Two of Dinah's twelve brothers, however, tricked the Hivites, murdered Shechem, and rescued Dinah.

Motivating Movement

1. First, list with the dancers the body postures and kinds of gestures which express loneliness and isolation. Some examples are:
    a. Head bent down and body curved over
    b. A repeated gesture, such as rocking or tracing a line on the ground with either a finger or a toe
    c. Walking aimlessly
    Next, put on some soft music and ask the dancers to explore movement which expresses loneliness and isolation. Works by Ravel and Satie are especially good for this purpose.

2. Have the group form a circle, all facing the center, and explore the different unison movement that is possible while maintaining the shape of a circle. Some examples are: expanding, contracting, revolving, sinking, and rising.

   Conclude the movement exploration by exploring the patterns that two concentric circles can make. The outer circle makes movements which are in spatial contrast to those of the inner circle. (The ideas for circle exploration come from *Materials of Dance as a Creative Art Activity* by Barbara Mettler, Mettler Studios, Tucson, Arizona, 1960, 220–221.)

Dance Midrash

Have one person portray Dinah while the rest portray the daughters of the land. The daughters of the land begin a circular dance. Dinah slowly enters the improvisation, first moving outside of the circle and then gradually joining the circle. The Dance Midrash continues until Dinah establishes that she is part of the group.

Making Connections

Together, read the rest of Dinah's story (Genesis 34:1–31). Lead a discussion centered on questions the story raises. Some examples are:

    Why did Dinah go out to join the daughters of the land?
    Were her brothers justified in their actions?
    What is Jacob's role in the story?

Relate the story to today by asking what Dinah's need to join the daughters tells us about women today. What kind of revengeful actions are around us? How does Jacob and Dinah's relationship help us understand contemporary father/daughter relationships?

Challenge

1. Dinah's reaction to her rape and to her brothers' actions are never told in the Genesis story. Have dancers create solos based on how Dinah might have felt and reacted. Encourage each person to have his/her own interpretation. An interesting way to present the solos is to read Genesis 34:1–31 and, when a place for Dinah's reaction occurs, stop and let a dancer portray what Dinah's reactions might have been.
2. One traditional interpretation of why Dinah went out to join the daughters is that she wanted to see their pagan rituals. In order to understand

better the society around the Israelites and how different their form of worship was, have the group create a circle dance which is inspired by the ancient goddess religions. Some books for ideas are:

> Starhawk. *The Spiral Dance: A Rebirth of the Ancient Religion of the Great Goddess.* New York: Harper and Row Publishers, 1979.
>
> Wolkstein, Diane, and Kramer, Samuel Noah. *Inanna: Queen of Heaven and Earth.* New York: Harper and Row, 1983.

Genesis
Advanced ■ ■ ■

Isaac Dies

> Isaac was a hundred and eighty years old when he breathed his last and died. He was gathered to his kin in ripe old age; and he was buried by his sons Esau and Jacob. (Genesis 35:28–29)

Description

Jacob and Esau struggled with each other from the womb. Jacob cheated Esau of his birthright and fled from him out of fear. Although they met again as adults, they did not stay in close contact. Yet, when their father died, they came together to bury him.

Motivating Movement

1. Develop movement phrases which require cooperative action. Some examples are: several people moving a heavy box together; three people jumping rope, two holding the rope while one jumps; and two people using a big saw to saw down a tree. First focus on the task. Then do the phrases again, only this time ask the group to pretend they don't like each other while doing the movement.

Making Connections

Ask the group to share experiences they have had in which a family member's death brought people closer together.

Dance Midrash

Jacob and Esau were no longer enemies when their father died. Their past however had been filled with much hostility. There were emotional interactions both with each other and with their father.

Divide the group into pairs. One person will portray Jacob and the other Esau. Ask them to create a dance of comforting each other at their father's death while sharing in movement their memories of interactions with each other and their parents. The important part of this Dance Midrash is that in spite of their history, they are both respectful to Isaac by coming together to bury him. Keep in mind that Esau was the son favored by Isaac, and that it was through Rebecca's cunning that Jacob received his father's blessing.

Challenge

Nine verses before Jacob buried his father, he buried Rachel, his favorite wife, who had died in childbirth. Jacob erected a pillar where Rachel was buried. Between the two burials, the twelve sons of Jacob were named. Improvise a dance, perhaps using the *Kaddish* prayer as accompaniment, which shows how Jacob felt at each burial.

Genesis
Beginner ■ □ □

Joseph Dreams

> *There we were binding sheaves in the field, when suddenly my sheaf stood up and remained upright, then your sheaves gathered around and bowed low to my sheaf.* (Genesis 37:7)

Description

It was obvious to Joseph's brothers that their father loved Joseph the most. When Joseph told them his dream about the sheaves, their jealousy and hatred of Joseph grew. In response to Joseph's dream, they asked, "Do you mean to rule over us?"

Motivating Movement

1. The dancers disperse throughout the space. One dancer circles the rest imagining he or she is trying to bind the group together. The dancer moves as if he or she is winding an invisible rope around and around them. The dancers who are being bound respond by moving closer together.
2. The group begins in a circle. The starting position for all the dancers is one of hunched-over shoulders, lowered head and eyes. One dancer begins by standing up in the straightest, highest position possible, even onto tiptoes with arms stretched overhead. As that dancer is straightening, the others bow low to the ground. Gradually return to the starting

position as the next dancer around the circle prepares to stand straight. Repeat around the circle.

Making Connections

Have dancers imagine this scenario: A family is struggling with a serious problem—financial, deception, violence, addiction, etc. Although tensions are high, they agree to sit down together to try to work things through.

Suddenly one member of the family stands up and, assuming a dominating tone of voice, tells the others he/she will no longer participate in the discussion. How do other family members react to the one who arrogantly tries to dominate? Do participants recognize the scenario as one which they have witnessed?

Joseph in his dream saw himself trying to work together with his brothers (binding sheaves) when suddenly his sheaf (representing him) stood upright and dominated the others. The brothers' reaction was anger and even hatred.

Dance Midrash

There are three parts to the improvisation:

Dancers move in ways that suggest they are both binding others (toward a cluster in the center) and being bound as brothers.

The dream section: When the dancers are clustered together, a dancer playing Joseph moves away aggressively and arrogantly from his brothers. The brothers move in ways that suggest humility and servitude.

The brothers then react to Joseph's dream. Their movement should reveal anger and hostility toward Joseph.

Challenge

1. Have dancers consider verse 37:9: "Look, I have dreamed another dream: And this time the sun, the moon, and eleven stars were bowing down to me." Create a Dance Midrash using this material.
2. Have dancers make up another dream Joseph may have shared with his brothers. What would be the images and symbols of this dream? Create a Dance Midrash using this creative material.

Genesis
Intermediate ■ ■ ☐

Joseph Is Cast into the Pit

> When Joseph came up to his brothers they stripped Joseph of his tunic, the ornamented tunic he was wearing, and took him and cast him into the pit. The pit was empty; there was no water in it.
> (Genesis 37:23–24)

Description

Jacob was sent to spy on his brothers who were away tending sheep. When the brothers saw Joseph approaching, they conspired to kill him. Reuben persuaded them to throw Joseph into a pit instead.

Motivating Movement

1. Have dancers define a circle around themselves, with a diameter of approximately 6'. They are to stay within the circle and improvise the following:
   a. Frustration and anger at being confined to the limited space
   b. Fear that they cannot ever go beyond the circle
   c. Comfort that they have retreated to this small space, which is a protecting circle
2. Coach dancers to explore movement in each of the defined situations through changes in posture, e.g., standing, kneeling, sitting, and lying.

Making Connections

Point out that sometimes the mood we are in and our outlook toward life affect how we perceive the things around us, e.g., some see a glass of water half full and some half empty. Ask each person to reflect on how he/she would perceive such a glass of water. Ask how he/she thinks Joseph would perceive the glass, and to provide supporting evidence for his/her answer.

Dance Midrash

Divide the group into quintets. One person in each quintet is Joseph. The others are to make a circle around Joseph, becoming the walls of the pit. Joseph is to dance the emotions he feels after he is thrown into the pit. The walls are to intensify the emotions that Joseph experiences. For example:

Joseph expresses fear—the walls tremble and shake.

Joseph curls up trying to go to sleep—the walls rock him to sleep.

Joseph prays to God to help him to get out of the pit—the walls pray (*daven*) with him.

Change parts until each person has had a chance to be Joseph.

Challenge

1. This exercise is a challenge for a mature group, particularly adults who have strong dance backgrounds. Working in small groups with one person portraying Joseph and the others the brothers, have each group choreograph a movement phrase which represents "casting him into the pit." The goal is to find movement that captures the intensity of the moment while being safe to do.
2. Divide the participants into small groups. Ask each group to outline a dream that Joseph might have had while he was in the pit. Have the groups dance the dream for each other. Some possibilities are:

    Angels from God bring Joseph wings and help him to fly out of the pit.

    A cloud floats over the pit and causes it to rain so that Joseph will have water to drink. The sun comes out and forms a rainbow with one end reaching into the pit so that Joseph can use the rainbow as a ladder.

    Joseph gets revenge on his brothers by casting them into fire.

    Joseph sees himself endlessly falling into deeper and deeper pits.

Genesis
Advanced ■ ■ ■

Judah's Pledge to Tamar

And [Judah] said, "What pledge shall I give you?" [Tamar] replied, "Your seal and cord, and the staff which you carry." (Genesis 38:18)

Description

Judah chose Tamar as a wife for his son. But the son died before having children. By tradition, Tamar then married her husband's brother in order to carry on the family name. But the brother also died before children were born. Judah was hesitant to give his third son to Tamar. Tamar, disguised as a harlot, exacted a pledge from Judah and slept with him. She conceived. Later Tamar identified Judah as the man who slept with her by showing the seal and cord and staff. Judah realized Tamar was in the right since he hadn't wed his third son to her. (See Genesis 38.)

Motivating Movement

1. Have dancers choose three gestures and begin by doing the gestures several times. Have them then exaggerate and shape the gestures to make them their own. Their personalities should be "stamped" on each gesture. Examples of gestures:

   Waving

Tucking hair behind an ear
Saluting
Shrugging shoulders
Nodding the head
Hand motioning to enter or to go away

Dance Midrash

Divide the group into pairs. One person plays Judah, the other Tamar. Judah creates a gesture that becomes his "seal, cord, and staff." One pair carries out the following scenario as the other pairs watch: Judah gestures his seal, cord, and staff to Tamar. Tamar receives the gesture by repeating it and integrating her own personality into its expression.

Then the pairs who have been watching take the same gestures and, personalizing them, reenact the above interaction.

When all have finished, the Tamar of the first pair imagines that time has passed and she has conceived by Judah. She gestures Judah's seal, cord, and staff back to him in order to identify him. Judah "receives" them, repeating in a way that captures his surprise, shame, and regret. The other pairs now reenact Tamar returning the gesture and Judah receiving it. The whole Dance Midrash can be repeated until each pair has had a chance to initiate the gestures.

Making Connections

Discuss with the group how it feels to give someone an object (or personal information) for safekeeping, knowing that at some later time he/she will want it returned (or kept in confidence). How would it feel to have that object (or personal information) lorded over him/her at some later date? Is it ever right to take an entrusted object and use it against a person? Was Tamar right in using Judah's seal, cord, and staff against him? What are the boundaries in using what belongs to another against him/her? Considerations might include self-defense, following the law, revenge.

Challenge

Everyone in the group chooses to be either Judah or Tamar. They are to create solo dances in which each presents his/her side of the story. Encourage everyone to use imagination in filling in details about what happened. A review of Genesis 38 would be very helpful.

Genesis
Beginner ■ □ □

Joseph in Charge

> *Pharaoh then gave Joseph the name Zaphenath-Paneah; and he gave him for a wife Asenath daughter of Poti-Phera, priest of On. Thus Joseph emerged in charge of the land of Egypt.* (Genesis 41:45)

Description

When none of Pharaoh's magicians were able to interpret his dreams, Pharaoh was told of Joseph's skill. Joseph was rushed from the prison, interpreted Pharaoh's dreams, and was rewarded with jewelry, fine clothes, a new name, a wife, and a position of power.

Motivating Movement

1. Have the group practice four basic ways of moving:
   Sustained
   Staccato
   Percussive
   Swinging
2. For leaders and groups with strong dance backgrounds, have the group practice different styles of moving:
   Balletic
   Folk
   Jazz

Different modern styles such as Graham, Cunningham, and postmodern

Dance Midrash

One person is Joseph and the rest are Egyptians. The group decides on a style or a basic way of moving from the "Motivating Movement" section above. Once the group's manner of moving is clearly established, Joseph enters and tentatively begins to move in the same way as the group. Gradually, he is able to move like everyone else, eventually becoming the leader of the group, and refining the movement. Repeat with different people portraying Joseph and with different styles or ways of moving for the Egyptians.

Making Connections

Ask each person to think of a way he/she, or someone he/she knows, is like Joseph (having mastered the customs of, and even becoming a leader of, the "secular" society). For example, an education provides entry into jobs that once were not open to Jews. Once in the job, a person may excel and be promoted to a higher level position. Share the advantages and disadvantages of being able to do this. (For example, an advantage would be improved economic level, while a disadvantage might be loss of cultural identity because of requirements to work on Shabbat and holidays.)

Challenge

When Joseph sees his brothers (see Genesis 42:6–8), he recognizes them even though they don't recognize him. Have the group expand on this moment. They can focus on the possibility that as Joseph sees his brothers, his "roots" (tradition and past) become important to him again in spite of his assimilation. Develop movement which shows how his past culture and family experiences begin to interplay with his current Egyptian assimilation. Two possibilities include:

Nomadic life compared with urban Egyptian life

His status as Jacob's favorite son and his current position of being second to Pharaoh

Genesis
Intermediate ■ ■ □

Joseph Names His Sons

Joseph named the first born Manasseh, meaning, "God has made me forget completely my hardship and my parental home." And the second he named Ephraim, meaning, "God has made me fertile in the land of my affliction." (Genesis 41:51–52)

Description

After successfully interpreting Pharaoh's dream about seven years of plenty and seven years of famine, Joseph was appointed vizier by Pharaoh. Pharaoh gave Joseph an Egyptian name and a wife. Joseph and his wife Asenath had two sons, Manasseh and Ephraim, born during the seven years of plenty.

Motivating Movement

1. Have the group explore "opposites" in movement. Some examples are:

low movement	high movement
fast	slow
big	small
stiff/rigid	flowing
straight shapes	round shapes
staccato	sustained

2. Have the group explore the dynamics of going from one type of movement to its opposite and then back to the original. For example, begin

moving slowly, gradually get faster, move in a fast tempo for a while and conclude by abruptly going back to moving slowly.

Dance Midrash

In the naming of his sons, Joseph tells a lot about himself. The name of each son represents an important aspect of Joseph's personality. Both aspects involve opposites.

Begin by having the group explore in dance Joseph's conflicted attempts to forget his past hardship and parental home, while at the same time remembering the past. One possible format is to have one person portray Joseph and the other members of the group to be people from his past, such as his brothers, father, prison keeper, etc. When Joseph is forgetting them, he may move them to the very edge of the dance space and ignore their presence. This can be contrasted with his act of remembering when he may choose to interact with the various characters based on the memories the characters elicit. Another format is to have everyone do a solo improvisation about Joseph interacting or ignoring/pushing away/forgetting imaginary characters from his past.

When the group has realized the dynamics of forgetting and remembering, progress to exploring the idea that God made Joseph fertile in the land of his affliction. In dance, portray Joseph as a slave, stranger, and prisoner in Egypt contrasted with his role as vizier in charge of all the land of Egypt.

Making Connections

Studying the character of Joseph provides an opportunity to reflect on our own strengths and weaknesses. On the positive side, Joseph was able to turn situations to his advantage. Ask the group for examples of times they have turned something that started out negatively into something positive.

Discuss the advantages and disadvantages of forgetting "hard times" in our own lives. Is it possible to forget completely? What is the effect of the passage of time on remembering hardships?

Challenge

In spite of the fact that Joseph had been removed from his parental home for many years, he immediately recognized his brothers, though he did not reveal his identity to them right away. It appears he was experiencing a number of different emotions upon seeing them. Together, read Genesis 42:6–26 and list the different emotions and reactions that Joseph might have had. After the list is complete, assign members of the group to each of the emotions/reactions. Have the group dance together their assigned emotions/reactions. Coaching ideas for this improvisation include reminding the dancers to:

Strongly portray their assigned emotion/reaction.

Interact in appropriate ways with other dancers by showing how other dancers' emotions/reactions affect them. (Do the other dancers' emotions/reactions cause conflict or harmony with the emotion/reaction he/she is portraying?)

Genesis
Intermediate ■ ■ ☐

Egyptians Become Serfs

And they said, "You have saved our lives! We are grateful to my lord [Joseph], and we shall be serfs to Pharaoh." (Genesis 47:25)

Description

The Egyptians were "grateful" to Joseph because he gave them bread and seed during a time of famine. In return, their farmland became the property of Pharaoh and they became Pharaoh's serfs.

Motivating Movement

1. Participants dance as if they are sated and happy as at a wedding banquet. Lively wedding music can accompany this exercise.
2. Participants imagine there is a famine. They are on a journey to a place far away at which there is supposed to be a distribution of food. Their movement should reflect hunger and exhaustion.
3. The group spreads out into a wide circle. The first person moves to a position suggesting slavery. The second person takes the same position as the first and then moves to a new position suggesting freedom. The third person begins in the "freedom" position in which the second person ended,

and moves to a different position suggesting slavery. Continue this pattern until everyone has had several opportunities to move.

Dance Midrash

The Egyptians were grateful that their lives had been saved; however, they now were serfs. Dancers imagine they are Egyptians and improvise the following stages:
- Hunger and uncertainty
- Approaching Joseph for help
- Satisfaction of hunger and appreciation
- The experience of being serfs, toiling for endless years

Making Connections

Have the group discuss what contrast they experienced between the last two stages above. What did the Egyptians have to give up in order to satisfy their hunger? How might the Egyptians have felt about their new status as serfs? What are some of the things people today give up in order to satisfy basic needs? Under what circumstances might people give up their:
- Dignity
- Freedom of speech
- Freedom to travel
- Citizenship

Challenge

Ask the dancers what freedoms they value most in their lives. Examples are freedom of speech, freedom to travel, freedom of thought, freedom to be represented in court, freedom to pursue an education, etc. The dancers improvise on giving up one of these precious freedoms.

Genesis
Intermediate ■ ■ □

Blessing Ephraim & Manasseh

> So he blessed them that day, saying, "By you shall Israel [Jacob] invoke blessings, saying: God make you like Ephraim and Manasseh." Thus he put Ephraim before Manasseh. (Genesis 48:20)

Description

Jacob blessed Joseph's sons, Ephraim and Manasseh. Manasseh was Joseph's firstborn and thus prime heir. Despite this, Jacob placed his hands on the children's heads in a crossed position, putting his right hand on Ephraim's head and his left on Manasseh's head. By so doing, he designated Ephraim as the recipient of the more favorable blessing.

Motivating Movement

1. Have dancers travel across the space moving:
    a. From one crossed position to another
    b. From one open position to another
    c. From crossed to open to crossed positions
    d. While keeping part of the body open and another part crossed

2. Have dancers practice movement which appears to be moving one way, then suddenly switches. Examples of movement switches are:
   a. High to low
   b. Forward to back, side to side
   c. Slow to fast
   d. Curving to zigzagging
   e. Stiff to loose
3. Ask dancers to come up with a quality they would use in blessing a child using the formula: "May God make you as Ephraim and Manasseh." Have each dancer improvise on his/her quality in front of the rest of the group, which tries to guess the quality being expressed by the performer. Qualities to consider are: strong, kind, free-thinking, compassionate, wise, etc.

Dance Midrash

In this improvisation dancers imagine that each is Jacob blessing the children. As they dance, they explore why Jacob crossed his hands, putting Ephraim before Manasseh. Do the improvisation twice, using the following possibilities as Jacob's motivation for switching from the expected.

Jacob's memory of his father Isaac: Jacob remembers how his father blessed him, the younger son, instead of Esau, the elder. In the case of Isaac, it was unclear whether or not he was aware of which son he was blessing. However, Jacob's switch is more explicitly intentional. Dancers seek to express how Jacob's memory of his father influenced his actions.

A premonition about the future: Jacob feels a special bond to Ephraim, intuiting that he is the one who has the qualities necessary to become the greater nation.

Making Connections

Ephraim and Manasseh both become great tribes. Talk about other biblical characters and some qualities each had which would inspire the group to want to invoke their names when making a blessing. Examples are Aaron, who was much beloved by the people; Moses, who exhibited great leadership qualities; Rebekah, who was generous and clever; Bezalel, who was artistic; Deborah, who was wise in judgment, and so on. Then, ask what qualities of contemporary figures are worthy of invoking when blessing another.

Challenge

1. Have each person choose a biblical character and create a solo in which he/she dances a blessing incorporating several of the admirable qualities of that character. Have dancers share their solos with each other.
2. Have each person choose a contemporary figure and create a solo in which he/she dances a blessing incorporating several of the admirable qualities of the person. Have dancers share their solos with each other.

Genesis
Advanced ■ ■ ■

Joseph Mourns His Father

> *When they came to Goren Ha-Atad, which is beyond the Jordan, they held there a very great solemn lamentation; and he observed a mourning period of seven days for his father.*
> (Genesis 50:10)

Description

When Jacob died, Joseph took the body to Canaan to bury him. He was accompanied by the officials of Pharaoh, the senior members of his court, all of Egypt's dignitaries, together with all of Joseph's household, his brothers, and his father's household. After great lamentation, Joseph observed seven days of mourning.

Motivating Movement

1. Have the dancers lie on the floor. Ask them to imagine a "sob" traveling through their bodies, beginning from their "centers" (the "pits of their stomachs"), proceeding through their upper bodies, until the sob is felt through their whole selves. Repeat, having the dancers stand, and repeat again with them moving in the space. Also, have the dancers experiment with initiating the sob from different parts of their bodies (e.g., beginning in their heads and traveling to their feet).

Making Connections

Ask participants to think of a time when they reacted physically to bad news. What exactly did they feel in their bodies? What "movements" were involved in their reactions? Note the Jewish practice of *"kria,"* rending a garment (or a symbolic ribbon), to express grief at the graveside.

Dance Midrash

There is linguistic evidence supporting the idea that the lamentation (*misped* in Hebrew) was a type of mourning dance. Dancers improvise on how they imagine this dance might have looked. Remind them that the feelings of grief expressed in a "lamentation dance" in biblical times would be similar to whatever feelings we might have at a funeral in our own day.

Challenge

Besides a "great and solemn lamentation," the verse refers to seven days of mourning. When in Numbers 20:29 it refers to Aaron's death, the text says, "...all the house of Israel bewailed Aaron thirty days." Then in Deuteronomy 34:8, the text says, "And the Israelites bewailed Moses in the steppes of Moab for thirty days." These verses inspired the stages of mourning observed in Judaism today:

Funeral

Shiva, seven days of mourning (for a parent, spouse, sibling, or son/daughter)

Sheloshim, a thirty-day period of less intense mourning

For more information regarding these stages, see *The Jewish Way in Death and Mourning* by Maurice Lamm (New York: Jonathan David, 1969). These stages allow mourners to feel and express their grief while gradually bringing them back to functioning in everyday life.

Have dancers improvise a dance in which they gradually move from intense grief to "normalcy." While all the dancers are to be mourners, they should feel free to make transitions between that role and the role of comforter.

Exodus

Exodus
Intermediate ■ ■ □

A New Pharaoh Deals Harshly

Let us deal shrewdly with them. (Exodus 1:10)

Description

At the beginning of the Book of Exodus, Joseph died and a new Pharaoh, who did not know Joseph, ruled over Egypt. Pharaoh told the Egyptian people that there were too many Israelites and that he intended to "deal shrewdly" with them.

Motivating Movement

1. Bring in pictures of early Egyptian architecture and art. Point out their formal, direct, and planar (two-dimensional) lines.
   a. Have the group practice very angular, planar, and stark movements representing Egyptian art.
   b. Create a sculpture of several figures by having one person take a shape, then another join in, until four or five people are making a composition together. Ask them to move together slowly, maintaining very angular and planar movements.

Dance Midrash

The quote from Torah, "Let us deal shrewdly with them," implies that the new Pharaoh had to teach the Egyptians to dislike the Israelites, and to be more forceful as masters over their Israelite slaves.

Have one person be Pharaoh. Pharaoh uses taut and stark movements to convince the rest of the group, who are Egyptians, to deal harshly with the Israelites. Perhaps some members of the group are reluctant to do so and even question Pharaoh's attitude. Pharaoh remains firm in his position until the whole group agrees with him.

Making Connections

Together, define the word "prejudice" and ask participants to share examples of prejudices they were taught. Ask if the information was given to them directly or indirectly. When and how did they become aware they were operating from a prejudicial point of view? Were they able to stop behaving in a prejudiced manner once they realized they were operating from such a point of view?

Challenge

1. Have each person imagine that he/she is an Israelite slave who hears Pharaoh telling the Egyptians to deal shrewdly with the Israelites. Create a dance which reveals how the Israelite slave might have reacted. Some possibilities are:

    Fear of how he/she might be mistreated

    Determination to prove his/her value

    Desire to escape

    Discouragement and resignation to the bleakness of the situation

2. Have the group create with their bodies a series of "sculptures" (frozen positions) in the Egyptian style, each sculpture depicting a relationship between an Egyptian master and Israelite slaves. The first sculpture shows a positive working relationship between the master and slaves. By the last sculpture, the Israelites are being treated inhumanly by the Egyptian master.
3. The following challenge is recommended for an older group and may be done for Yom Hashoah (Holocaust Memorial Day). Prior to the time of Hitler, Jews were comfortable and secure in Germany. Once Hitler came to power, they began to lose their rights as citizens. They were restricted

in trade and travel. They were sent to concentration camps and millions were killed. Have the group imagine they are prosperous, comfortable German Jews. They are to improvise a dance which illustrates the effects of Nazi rule, beginning with the lesser restrictions and ending in confinement and destruction.

Exodus
Beginner ■ □ □

The Burning Bush

There was a bush all aflame, yet the bush was not consumed. (Exodus 3:2)

Description

Moses was tending the sheep of his father-in-law when a burning bush captured his attention. Although the bush burned, it was not consumed. God spoke to him out of the bush.

Motivating Movement

1. Call out each of the words or phrases in the following list. Ask dancers to put the word or phrase into movement. Give them several minutes to explore each word or phrase.
   Blazing
   Flames leaping
   Simmering and crackling
   To become ignited
   Glow

Dance Midrash

Have dancers portray Moses at the moment the burning bush captures his attention. As they expand on that moment, have dancers focus on Moses' realization that the burning bush not only is an external sign of God, but also signals the beginning of his own internal "fire." It is this internal fire or passion that will enable Moses to lead the Israelites.

Making Connections

Ask the group to describe times they have become "fired up" with an idea. How do they recognize that they are fired up? How do they handle this energy? Discuss the positive and negative aspects of being fired up.

Challenge

As a group, read Exodus 3:2 to 4:17. These verses reveal that Moses is reluctant to lead the Israelites. In order to "ignite" Moses into action, God reassured him with additional signs. God turned Moses' rod into a snake and then back into a rod, and made leprosy appear and disappear on Moses' hands.

All the dancers are to portray Moses as he comes to terms with his leadership role. The improvisation might have the following progression:

Moses realizes he has been chosen leader of the Israelites.

Moses reveals his doubts at being able to lead the Israelites.

The signs of God reinforce the "fire" within Moses.

Moses decides to move forward as leader of the Israelites.

Note: The above challenge is similar to the "Dance Midrash" sections of "Let My People Go" on page 74 and "Moses' Impediment" on page 77, as well as to the "Challenge" section of "Moses' Final Address" on page 197.

Exodus
Beginner ■ ☐ ☐

Moses Stands on Holy Ground

Remove your sandals from your feet, for the place on which you stand is holy ground.
(Exodus 3:5)

Description

Moses' attention was drawn to the burning bush. God spoke to him from the bush and told him to remove his sandals because the ground on which he stood was holy.

Motivating Movement
1. Ask dancers to dance barefoot, especially if they do not dance regularly in bare feet. (It is highly recommended that they do regularly work in bare feet.)
2. Ask dancers to imagine that they are dancing in the following places:
    a. At the beach—running, playing, tracing patterns with their feet in the sand, and occasionally wading in the water
    b. Walking barefoot in a nice grassy field
    c. Running barefoot across a stony field
    d. Hopping across an asphalt parking lot on a hot summer day

Dance Midrash

Each person is to imagine that he/she is Moses. Moses takes off his sandals and stands, walks, and finally dances, acknowledging the holiness of the ground on which he is standing.

Making Connections

Lead a discussion about what makes a place spiritual or holy. Ask participants to share times when they felt spiritual because of where they were. Ask if they have ever been to a place that they felt was ordinary, only to experience spiritual feelings later in the same place.

Challenge

1. Moses was told by God that the ground on which he stood was holy. In contrast, Jacob (see Genesis 28:17) awoke very shaken after his dream of angels ascending and descending a stairway. He said, "How awesome is this place. This is none other than the abode of God."
    Ask the group to dance Jacob waking up and acknowledging that the place he is in is sacred. Build particularly on the differences between the reaction of Moses and that of Jacob.
    Conclude by asking the participants to imagine they are alone in a familiar place. They begin to sense that the place has taken on a new, sacred dimension. Create a dance showing this.
2. An alternate challenge: The idea that a place is sacred or holy is also illustrated in the words of the following traditional American Indian song. Have the group choreograph a dance to these words:
    Where we sit is holy
    Holy is the ground.
    Forest, mountain, river
    Listen to the sound.
    Great spirit circling
    All around.

Exodus
Intermediate ■ ■ □

Let My People Go

Moses and Aaron went and said to Pharaoh, "Thus says the Lord, the God of Israel: Let my people go." (Exodus 5:1)

Description

Moses was instructed by God to appear before Pharaoh on behalf of the Israelites. He reluctantly agreed to do so once Aaron's help was enlisted. Moses and Aaron gathered together the elders of the Israelites. Moses performed for the elders the signs God had shown him and thus gained their support. The two brothers then went to Pharaoh for the first time.

Motivating Movement

1. Teach the group a simple pattern such as 3 steps, followed by a turn, ending with a balance on one foot. As a group, practice the pattern several times. Have each person do the phrase alone, the first time conveying reluctance and the second time confidence.

Making Connections

Ask each person to share times when he/she knew it was important to do something, but lacked confidence. How did each individual overcome this lack of confidence? What role did other people play in helping them to gain confidence?

Dance Midrash

This Dance Midrash is especially appropriate for Pesach. Divide the group into pairs. One person in each pair is Moses and the other is Aaron.

Together they are to create a dance of coming before Pharaoh and making their request to "let my people go." Coach the pairs to work on how Aaron might help Moses to overcome his initial reluctance.

Note: This Dance Midrash is similar to the "Dance Midrash" section of "Moses' Impediment" (see page 77) and the "Challenge" sections of "The Burning Bush" (see page 71) and "Moses' Final Address" (see page 197).

Challenge

James Weldon Johnson, a Black American poet of the 20s, retells the Exodus story in his poem "Let My People Go" (*God's Trombones: Seven Negro Sermons in Verse*, New York: Viking Press, 1927). In many ways, Johnson's retelling of the Exodus story is a parallel description of the experiences of American Black slaves. Invite a group from a neighboring Black church to join you for a special session. Together, explore Johnson's poem in movement improvisations from each of your respective cultural points of view. The leaders of both groups should meet prior to the session to go over the poem and to choose the key moments/movements on which to focus.

The poem can also be developed into a dance/theatre piece by the combined groups and presented to their respective communities.

Exodus
Advanced ■ ■ ■

Moses' Impediment

> *But Moses appealed to the Lord saying, "The Israelites would not listen to me; how then should Pharaoh heed me, a man of impeded speech!"* (Exodus 6:12)

Description

Moses expressed insecurity about asserting a position of leadership because of his speech impediment. (He previously expressed this concern in Exodus 4:10 when God called upon him to be the leader of the Israelite people.) In this passage Moses was concerned about being the one to approach Pharaoh to demand that the Israelites be allowed to leave Egypt.

Motivating Movement

1. Have dancers practice confident versus insecure movements.
2. Dancers are to experience a physical difficulty or "impediment." Have them:
    a. Move through the space using only one leg.
    b. Move through the space without using legs at all.
    c. Transport an object (such as a chair) across the space using only one arm.
    d. Transport an object across the space without using arms at all.

3. Have each dancer create a short phrase of movement. Coach dancers to be specific in terms of choreographing the rhythm, movement quality, and emotional expression. When each dancer has his/her phrase, divide the group into pairs. Have dancers teach their partners their phrase without using words to explain.

Making Connections

Lead a discussion about individuals who accomplished great things despite some kind of physical difficulty. Examples include: Franklin Delano Roosevelt (who was restricted to a wheelchair), Beethoven (who composed symphonies when he was deaf), and Franz Rosenzweig (who in the last days of his illness dictated a book to his wife by blinking his eyes). Ask the group to share their thoughts about individuals who have led inspiring lives despite an "impediment." Ask why they think God chose Moses to be the leader of the Israelites despite his speech impediment.

Dance Midrash

Divide the group into pairs. One person is Moses, the other is Pharaoh. Moses wants to convince Pharaoh to let the Israelites depart Egypt. Moses makes Pharaoh understand his demand by communicating through a phrase of movement. The movement phrase is to be choreographed beforehand by the dancer playing Moses. (Since the dancers will switch roles, both partners can choreograph their Moses phrase at the same time, before the actual improvisation begins.) This improvisation is an example of a Dance Midrash which elaborates on one small idea in the verse (that of Moses' speaking difficulty), and takes it to an extreme (so that Moses doesn't use speech at all).

The improvisation begins with Moses preparing himself to approach Pharaoh. When they meet, Moses makes his request understood to Pharaoh by teaching him his phrase. Moses teaches without using words. When Pharaoh learns the phrase, Moses departs from his presence. Switch roles and repeat.

Note: This Dance Midrash complements and represents another angle on issues similar to those in the preceding Dance Midrash and in the "Challenge" sections of "The Burning Bush" (see page 71) and "Moses' Final Address" (see page 197).

Challenge

Moses referred to his speech impediment several times (Exodus 4:10, 6:12, and 6:30). He demurred several times before he was finally able to overcome the lack of confidence caused by his impediment. Despite his initial hesitancy, he went on to become a great leader.

Have dancers improvise a dance in which they struggle to overcome some kind of personal difficulty. Coach dancers to consider not only physical difficulties, but those related to personality, social skills, and learning as well. Have them explore the ups and downs involved in building the confidence necessary to rise above the difficulty and move forward with strength.

Exodus
Beginner ■ □ □

Frogs Everywhere

Aaron held out his arm over the waters of Egypt, and the frogs came up and covered the land of Egypt. (Exodus 8:2)

Description

Frogs were the second plague brought upon the Egyptians because Pharaoh wouldn't let the enslaved Israelites go.

Motivating Movement

1. Have dancers explore all kinds of jumps: low to the ground, high, going up on one foot and landing on two, with a turn in the air, etc.

Dance Midrash

Half of the dancers are frogs, half are Egyptians. The Egyptians begin by going about their daily business. After being motioned by the leader to come out of an imagined river, the frogs jump, doing their best to cover as much space as possible. The Egyptians try to carry on as well as they can. Switch roles.

Making Connections

Discuss with the group how they felt in the Dance Midrash above when they were being surrounded by frogs. In like manner, what kinds of problems prevent them from going about their own daily activity? If they were given an overload of those problems, how would they react?

Challenge

Create a dance that portrays a group of Egyptians going to Pharaoh, explaining and complaining to him what damage the plague of frogs is doing, and urging him to do something quickly. Elements of the dance should include:

- Fear and respect before Pharaoh
- Imitation of frog movements
- Movements expressing complaining, exasperation, and desperation
- Pleading with Pharaoh

Exodus
Beginner ■ □ □

Darkness Descends on Egypt

> Moses held out his arm toward the sky and thick darkness descended upon all the land of Egypt for three days. (Exodus 10:22)

Description

Darkness is the ninth plague brought upon the Egyptians to convince Pharaoh to let the Israelites go.

Motivating Movement

1. Use a very large piece of fabric. A parachute is ideal. (It is sometimes possible to get one from an Army/Navy store.) Have the group hold onto the edges of the fabric and move together, reacting to the fabric's movement and that of other group members.
2. Have the group link together (no fabric) by holding onto each other in unique ways. They are to move in a slow, sustained manner maintaining physical contact with each other.
3. Have the group improvise movement that conveys light and dark.
4. Have dancers portray their reactions to the light cycle in a day: sunrise, noon, sunset, twilight, moonlit night, and a night when there are no stars or moonlight.

Making Connections

Discuss the impact that the daylight has on us during the year. Point out the differences we might feel in the summer when the days are longer versus the winter when days are short. Ask if anyone has been in Alaska or another northern location with a midnight sun and what that is like. Ask the question, "How do we react emotionally to extremes of light and dark?"

Dance Midrash

Half the group is the thick darkness and the other half the Egyptians. The Egyptians are moving normally, carrying out daily tasks, when the thick darkness (either one massive group linked together or several smaller groups) enters and spreads an imaginary darkness over the space. The Egyptians become disoriented and separated from each other due to the darkness, and are no longer able to do their normal tasks. Coach the Egyptians to portray their disorientation, isolation, and any other emotions they might feel as the darkness continues to prevail. Repeat, changing parts.

Challenge

During the Passover *Seder*, it is customary for Jews to remove from their full cups a drop of wine for each plague. The full cups symbolize joy and abundance. This ritual is a symbolic way of diminishing joy as the suffering of the plagued Egyptians is remembered. Use this ritual of removing a drop of wine as a linking device for the group to choreograph the Ten Plagues (blood, frogs, lice, wild beasts, blight, boils, hail, locusts, darkness, and death of the firstborn). The actual recitation of the plagues as done at the *Seder* can serve as an accompaniment. The recitation can be repeated several times. Various percussion instruments, such as drums, cymbals, and bells, can be added as well. Also, masks can be created and used. This exercise is an excellent one to share with others or to include as part of a community *Seder*.

Exodus
Beginner ■ □ □

Leaving Egypt

> This is how you shall eat it: your loins girded, your sandals on your feet, and your staff in your hand, and you shall eat it hurriedly. It is a Passover offering to the Lord. (Exodus 12:11)

Description

The paschal lamb is offered each year as a commemoration of the first Passover. At that time, God smote the firstborn of the Egyptians, but passed over the homes of the Israelites which had been marked with the lamb's blood. This action was the tenth plague God carried out against the Egyptians, the plague that finally convinced Pharaoh to allow the Israelites to leave.

Motivating Movement

1. Ask dancers to imagine they are each holding a staff. Have them improvise movement inspired by images of the staff, such as the following:
   a. Symbol of power
   b. Symbol of dignity
   c. Support during times of physical exhaustion
   d. Support during times of emotional fatigue
   e. Object which steadies movement which is off balance

    f. Object which throws steady movement off balance
    g. Tool which prods and gathers together (in particular a flock of animals or a group of people)
2. Have the group begin dancing low to the ground using slow, quiet, and mundane movement. Coach them to expand gradually on their movement, building to a point at which the movement is fast, grand, frenzied, and covers much space.
3. Follow the dynamic outlined in #2 immediately above. This time, however, have dancers begin by pantomiming some of the detailed tasks involved in getting dressed, such as taking clothes out of closets and drawers, putting clothes on different parts of the body, fastening, buttoning, tying, smoothing away wrinkles, etc. Coach them to expand gradually on these tasks, building them until they become fast, grand, and frenzied dance movement.

Dance Midrash

Have dancers imagine they are Israelites and improvise on the theme of "getting ready." Incorporate movement based on girding, putting on shoes, and taking staff in hand. Incorporate into the improvisation feelings that might have been experienced by the Israelites as they ate hurriedly, such as fear, excitement, uncertainty, and/or faith. Also, remind dancers of the repulsion and confusion the Israelites may have felt since, while they carried out the Passover ritual, Egyptians (firstborn sons) were dying. There is a feeling of irony in this turn of events, as Pharaoh, just a few chapters ago, had commanded all newly born sons of the Israelites to be killed.

Making Connections

Have a few people describe their "ritual" of getting ready in the morning. Have them comment on what they think about as they carry out this routine. Then, have them compare and contrast what might be going through their minds if they knew that they were leaving not just for the day, but for good (moving away).

Challenge

When Ethiopian Jews have their Passover *Seder*, their tradition is to carry it out with loins girded, sandals on feet, and staff in hand. In other words, they recreate what is written in the Bible. Ask dancers to create movements appropriate to some of the *Seder* foods, rituals, and symbols.

Note: Traditional *Seder* foods are: hard boiled egg and roasted shankbone (symbols of abundance), parsley (symbol of spring), *charoset* (symbol of the mortar used by Israelite slaves), bitter herbs (symbol of the bitterness of slavery), salt water (symbol of tears), *matzah* (symbol of bread that did not have time to rise because the Israelites left in a hurry), wine (symbol of joy), and the cup of Elijah (symbol of future redemption).

Exodus
Advanced ■ ■ ■

Sign and Symbol of Freedom

And so it shall be a sign upon your hand and a symbol on your forehead that with a mighty hand God freed us from Egypt.
(Exodus 13:16)

Description

After the death of the Egyptian firstborn, Pharaoh quickly let the Israelites go. A break in the biblical narration then follows, during which ways of remembering God's deliverance of the Israelites are listed. These include the commandments in the above quotation which are repeated almost word for word twice in this same chapter (see Exodus 13:9).

Motivating Movement

1. Bring in *tefillin* and teach the participants how to put them on. When everyone is comfortable with the actual process of putting on *tefillin*, ask them to go through the process in pantomime. Next expand the pantomime gestures to dance movement.
2. Have the group experiment with other wrapping and binding movements directed toward wrapping and binding themselves.

Dance Midrash

Have the group imagine it is one year after the slaying of the Egyptian firstborn and that they are among the Israelites freed from slavery. Using the gestures learned to put on *tefillin*, have each person create a dance prayer that follows the command to remember how God freed the Israelites from slavery. Include in the dance prayer feelings of remembering recent slavery. Also, have the dancers keep in mind their current condition of wandering in the desert, and how this might influence their prayer.

Making Connections

Ask participants to think about prayer and the ritual connected with prayer. Ask the question: "Do gestures help in the act of prayer?" List different ritual gestures that go with prayer.

Challenge

The phrase "You shall love the Lord your God with all your might, with all your heart, with all your soul" is found in the early chapters of the Book of Exodus. In Hebrew it is called the *V'ahavta*.

As a group create a modern day dance prayer that is a reminder of past slavery and a celebration of freedom. In a Jewish setting, use the chanting of the *V'ahavta* as an accompaniment to your dance.

Option: Refine and polish the prayer and share it as part of a worship service.

Exodus
Beginner ■ ☐ ☐

Crossing the Sea

> And the Israelites went into the sea on dry ground, the waters
> forming a wall for them on their right and on their left.
> (Exodus 14:22)

Description

When Moses and the Israelites fled Egypt, they came to a seemingly insurmountable obstacle, the Red Sea. Moses was told by God to stretch his hand over the sea and that the waters would part. With the Egyptians not far behind, the Israelites passed through the sea on dry ground.

Motivating Movement

1. Play *Follow the Leader*, emphasizing active movement. For example, when the leader says "Go," the group swings their arms about freely and loosely. When the leader says "Stop," the group stops movement abruptly. Repeat several times, then repeat with legs, head, torso, hips, and whole body.
2. Give the group a large space to improvise a dance of freedom. As they dance, narrow the space in which they are allowed to "celebrate." Continue decreasing the space until the dancers have only a narrow aisle in which to move. After the dancers experience moving in the constricted

space, remove the imaginary barrier and allow them to move freely again throughout the whole space.

Dance Midrash

Designate a part of the space as water. Ask the group to be the Israelites excited by their escape from Egypt, but terrified by the sound of the Egyptians in the distance catching up with them. The Israelites come to the sea. In movement, explore reactions to the following:

The seeming dead end in front of them

The waters parting before their very eyes (do they plunge in, back away, hesitate?)

Moving through the sea on the dry land with a wall of water on each side of them

Making Connections

Have the group discuss "walls" in a more abstract way. What kinds of "walls" have they encountered in their lives? (Examples include a difficult loss, a painful memory, discrimination.) Ask the group to discuss or portray in dance the emotions they felt as they faced this "wall." Have them explore how their emotions changed as they moved beyond the wall or encountered another related hurdle.

Challenge

1. In Exodus 15:20 it says, "Miriam the prophetess, the sister of Aaron, took a timbrel in her hand; and all the women went out after her with timbrels and dances." Recreate Miriam's dance.
2. There is a Midrash about Nachshon, the first person to leap into the water after Moses raised his staff. He had such faith in God that even though he could not swim, he jumped in before he saw the waters part. Create a dance based on Nachshon and his incredible leap of faith.

Exodus
Intermediate ■ ■ ☐

Hands of Victory

Then whenever Moses held up his hand, Israel prevailed, but whenever he let down his hand, Amalek prevailed. (Exodus 17:11)

Description

The Israelites were at war with the Amalekites. Joshua led the Israelites in battle while Moses, Aaron, and Hur stationed themselves on top of a hill. When Moses lifted his hands, the Israelites prevailed. When his hands grew heavy, Aaron and Hur supported them so that they remained up until the sun set.

Motivating Movement

1. Choose one person as leader to stand on one side of the space. The rest of the dancers stand on the other side. When the leader raises his/her arms, dancers move swiftly forward; when the leader lowers his/her arms, dancers stop abruptly. The leader continues until dancers reach the place where he/she is standing. Take turns being leader.
2. Have dancers practice movements that capture the sense of "prevailing," and share them with each other. Possibilities include:
    a. Exalted movement such as leaps, open-armed turns, jumps, whirls, etc.

b. Aggressive movement such as kicks, thrusting arms forward, sharp elbow turns, etc.
c. Percussive movement such as marching, stomping, clapping, etc.

Dance Midrash

One person is Moses. Half of the rest of the group are Israelites and half are Amalekites. When Moses' hands are raised, the Israelites dance as if they are prevailing, and the Amalekites either stop moving or greatly lower the intensity of their movements. When Moses' hands are lowered, the opposite happens (the Amalekites prevail, and the Israelites stop or slow down).

The improvisation ends with Moses' hands remaining raised in a steady position. Whoever is Moses may choose to dance using even and steady movements while raising and lowering hands. Repeat, switching roles.

Making Connections

Ask dancers to think of a difficult experience or event in their lives. Examples are: a sports or academic competition, an upsetting argument or fight, an illness, a performance.

For the Israelites, Moses' hands may have symbolized steadfast faith, prayer, strength, or pride. Or, they might have symbolized a flag for the emerging Israelite nation. Have dancers compare their personal experiences with those of the Israelites. What enabled the dancers to get through their experiences? (What were their "hands aloft"?)

Challenge

1. Divide the group into pairs. One dancer is an Israelite soldier; the other is Moses, who symbolizes to the struggling soldier one of the following: faithfulness, strength, power, determination, pride, protection, etc.

   The soldier begins by improvising struggling movements. As the soldier and Moses interact, the soldier is inspired by Moses' influence. Gradually, the soldier's movement goes from struggling to prevailing. Switch roles and repeat.

2. The challenge is repeated using a contemporary person struggling with a contemporary problem and a contemporary Moses who embodies a quality which inspires the other to prevail.

Exodus
Beginner ■ □ □

Keep the Sabbath

Remember the Sabbath day and keep it holy. (Exodus 20:8)

Description

The verse above enjoins us to distinguish the Sabbath day from all other days of the week. It is the fourth commandment which God gave to the children of Israel.

Motivating Movement

Teach the traditional gestures which accompany the Sabbath candle lighting blessing—circling the flames and covering the eyes. Have the group expand the gesture into dance movement. First, do it very slowly, then make it as large as possible, involving the whole body in the circling of the flame and the covering of the eyes.

Making Connections

Discuss the key words in this verse. Ask how members of the group will remember or remind themselves when Sabbath comes. How do they think their grandparents or great grandparents kept the Sabbath? In what ways do we make the Sabbath separate or holy? Guide the group to focus on the specific prayers by which we usher in and end the Sabbath.

Dance Midrash

Divide the group. One half is the older generation, while the other half is a young generation. The youth are quietly watching the ritual of candle lighting done by the elders. The elders might come over and teach the youth, involving them in the ritual. Or, they might choose to be very mysterious about what they are doing. Reverse roles. Accompaniment for the improvisation can be the traditional blessing over the Sabbath candles repeated as many times as necessary.

Challenge

Abraham Heschel taught that Sabbath is a celebration of time rather than space. On the Sabbath day, said Heschel, we are called upon to "share in what is eternal time, from the results of creation to the mystery of creation, from the world of creation to the creation of the world."

Improvise a dance inspired by the idea of an eternal time reflecting the mystery of the creation and the creation of the world itself. Coach the group to use sustained and quiet movement and to become conscious of their own rhythm—their breathing and heartbeat.

This exercise is especially effective if done outside or at a retreat or camp where the sounds of nature can serve as background.

Exodus
Intermediate ■ ■ □

Amazement at Sinai

> All the people witnessed the thunder and lightning, the blare of the horn and the mountain smoking; and when the people saw it, they fell back and stood at a distance. (Exodus 20:15)

Description

The Ten Commandments had just been communicated to the people by Moses speaking in the name of God. The people were in awe because they had witnessed the Revelation.

Motivating Movement

1. Have dancers improvise movements based on their sensory responses to the following:
    a. A loud, irregular drum sound (thunder)
    b. Bright ribbons held and moved by the dancers (lightning)
    c. A blaring horn (preferably "live," although a recording will work)
    d. An imagined forest fire which surrounds them (mountain smoking)
2. Have dancers explore different ways of "falling back." Next have them experiment with falling back in awe and trembling.

Making Connections

All of the senses are involved in this verse: hearing the thunder and horns, seeing the lightning and smoke, tasting and smelling the smoke, and feeling the smoke (especially as it would sting the eyes). Talk about times when most or all of the senses might be stimulated, and how the group reacts to those situations. When are the situations pleasant, powerful, overwhelming? At what point are group members drawn in and at what point do they want to back off? Consider the following situations:

The eruption of a volcano
An amusement park on a hot, crowded day
A shopping mall during the holidays
A wedding reception
A baseball game

What made experiencing the Revelation at Sinai different from encountering any other event?

Dance Midrash

Ask dancers to imagine that they are at the foot of Mt. Sinai. They are to respond with all five senses to what is happening in the verse. Have them spend several minutes experiencing what is happening before they "fall back" (sometimes translated as "tremble") and "stand at a distance." Remind them to be aware of exactly how they might "fall back" ("tremble") and "stand at a distance."

Challenge

If there were to be a time of revelation today, where might it take place and how might that moment be experienced by witnesses? The dancers respond to these questions by creating a dance either individually or in small groups. Their movements should reveal what types of sights, sounds, smells, tastes, and feelings they would experience. After each dance is performed, have the viewers respond to what they thought the performers were experiencing. The performers can then share verbally the concept of revelation which they tried to convey.

Exodus
Intermediate ■ ■ □

Helping Your Enemy

> When you see the ass of your enemy lying under its burden and would refrain from raising it, you must nevertheless raise it with [your enemy]. (Exodus 23:5)

Description

This verse is included in a list of laws concerning property and interpersonal behavior. Many of these laws prohibit oppressing individuals who are in disadvantageous positions (e.g., strangers, orphans, widows, the poor, and those being judged in legal disputes).

Motivating Movement

1. Divide the group into pairs. Have the pairs practice showing antagonism and hostility to each other.
2. Have the group imagine that they must cooperate in order to lift a heavy burden. Begin with one person trying to lift the burden alone. Slowly, direct additional dancers one by one to assist in the process. Only when the last dancer adds his/her support should the burden be lifted completely. These are imaginary burdens to try to lift:
    a. A car in a snow drift
    b. A fallen telephone pole
    c. A treasure chest of coins at the bottom of the sea

3. Divide the group into pairs. One dancer tries to move across the space. The partner, while maintaining physical contact with the dancer, tries to impede the dancer's advance by giving him/her resistance. (The partner should not give so much resistance as to limit all movement.) Positions for the partner to try:
   a. Facing the dancer, fold arms, and lean against his/her chest.
   b. Facing the dancer, place hands on his/her hips.
   c. On the knees, facing the dancer, place hands on his/her hips.
   d. Provide resistance with shoulder, hip, or back.
4. For a more advanced group with experience dancing together: Ask dancers to resist tendencies to move in their own style, adopting instead the style of another dancer in the group. Have them improvise, using the "adopted" way of moving.

Making Connections

Lead a discussion on cooperating with enemies. Ask the group to come up with examples of times when antagonistic nations have had to cooperate in order to "lift a burden" (e.g., the banning of weapons, the cleaning up of pollutants, and the rescuing from extinction of endangered species). Talk about the effect of such cooperation on those who have joined together for a common purpose. How are attitudes changed? Bring the discussion to a more personal level, asking the group to share situations in which they cooperated with an "enemy." What was the effect? Were attitudes changed?

Dance Midrash

Divide the group into pairs. One partner is the owner of an animal trapped under its burden; the other is an enemy passing by. The improvisation begins with the owner struggling to raise his/her animal. The enemy enters and takes note of the scene. The pair continues by improvising together on the themes of enmity and resistance. Gradually, as the enemy decreases his/her resistance, the dancers redirect their hostile energy and cooperate in raising the animal. In summary, there are three parts to this improvisation:
   Setting the scene
   Enmity and resistance
   Redirection of hostile energy to cooperation

Challenge

Each dancer imagines himself/herself to be burdened with a specific problematic situation. This burden is to be like a physical impediment to his/her movement. In the improvisation the dancer gradually goes through a process of resisting his/her own "burden," then cooperating with it.

While the dancer should begin by using comfortable and familiar movement styles, by the end, the dancer's aim is to be moving comfortably and naturally in a style "new" to him/her.

Exodus
Advanced ■ ■ ■

Against Cruelty

You shall not boil a kid in its mother's milk. (Exodus 23:19;
Exodus 34:26; Deuteronomy 14:21)

Description

This verse conjures a picture of a vulnerable baby animal, the epitome of innocence, being subjected to the violence of being boiled to death in its mother's milk. While this injunction can be understood literally, it can also be seen as a condemnation of cruelty and torture.

Motivating Movement

1. Have dancers be water. Beginning at "room temperature," they go from heating, to simmering, to boiling.
2. Have dancers imagine they are at home in a room feeling comfortable and safe. They begin to feel the room grow warmer and warmer until it gradually becomes uncomfortable. Have them move in response to the heat as it becomes unbearable. Their movement may reflect panic, suffocation, collapse, etc.

Making Connections

Lead a discussion on cruelty and torture. Examples are: the clubbing to death of baby seals for their fur coats or the killing of elephants for their ivory tusks, Holocaust victims who were gassed to death in the countries in which they were born and raised, child abuse, religious cults that espouse murder or mass suicide.

Dance Midrash

Have dancers choose a circumstance in which cruelty and torture might be experienced, and improvise based on the feelings of a victim. After improvising on various circumstances, discuss which circumstance seems to come closest to the intention of the verse.

Challenge

The injunction cited above appears three times in the Bible. In Deuteronomy 14:21, the context is animals which are permitted and forbidden as food. The notion of not boiling a kid in its mother's milk gave rise to the injunction forbidding the mixing of milk and meat products. One interpretation is that life forces and death forces are not to be mixed.

Divide the group in half. One half is to be life forces and the other half is to be death forces. During the improvisation, dancers are to focus on how to develop the identity of their particular force and how to relate to, but not mix with, their opposite forces.

Exodus
Beginner ■ □ □

Giving

The Lord spoke to Moses, saying, "Tell the Israelite people to bring me gifts; you shall accept gifts for me from all persons whose heart so moves them." (Exodus 25:1–2)

Description

In the building of the Tabernacle, the furnishings were to be gifts provided by the people. The Israelites were asked to bring the raw materials which would be used to make the Ark, lampstand, curtain, and altar. Gold, silver, copper, yarns, spices, oils, skins, and wood were listed as raw materials.

Motivating Movement

1. Have the group experiment with movement representative of "giving," beginning from the center of the body and going outward. Contrast this movement with movement that begins outward and comes into the body, which is representative of "gathering." Bach's Brandenburg Concertos make wonderful accompaniment for this and help give the movement flow and energy.

Making Connections

Discuss the way we give and receive presents on birthdays and holidays. Point out the difference in feeling between choosing a meaningful gift for someone who is very special to us and the burden of giving a gift as an obligation. Talk about giving to charity and how we determine whom we give to and how much.

Dance Midrash

The acts of giving and receiving are both described in the verse quoted above. Have each person spend 5–10 minutes creating a phrase of giving that is 16 counts long and which he/she can repeat. (An example of a 16 count phrase: 4 steps forward, 4 counts reaching arms forward, 4 counts walking in a circle with arms still stretched forward, 4 counts raising arms overhead and opening to the side.) Point out that the finest materials were requested for the Tabernacle and that each person is to strive for the finest "giving" movement he/she can create. When everyone has his/her phrase, divide the group into pairs. Begin by having one person do his/her choreographed phrase to another person, who responds spontaneously to the movement with a receiving or gathering-in movement. Encourage the recipient to build the movement response based on the movement phrase observed. Repeat this several times so that the recipient has a real chance to react to the movement energy of the giver. Change roles and repeat.

Challenge

The emphasis in this verse is on "all whose heart so moves them." In other words, it took many people bringing gifts to make the furnishings, not merely one big contributor. The gifts also were complementary, each contributing to a part of the whole. Have the group build an improvisation of giving in which each person's movements are inspired by one of the items listed below. Each person keeps his/her unique quality based on the material he/she has chosen, while interacting with others in order to become part of a complete pattern.

The raw materials listed in the Bible are:

gold	goat's hair	lapis lazuli
silver	tanned ram skins	stones for setting
copper	dolphin skins	ephod
blue yarn	acacia wood	purple yarn
oil for lighting	breast piece	crimson yarn
spices for anointing oil	fine linen	aromatic incense

Exodus
Beginner ■ ☐ ☐

Winged Cherubim

The cherubim shall have their wings spread out above, shielding the cover with their wings. They shall confront each other, the faces of the cherubim being turned toward the cover. (Exodus 25:20)

Description

God told Moses how the Tabernacle was to be made and furnished. The details included instructions to place two cherubim of gold on top of the Ark cover.

Motivating Movement

1. Have dancers experiment with different kinds of arm and upper body movements. Talk about the different ways birds move their wings. Pictures of different birds in flight can help motivate movement. Have dancers improvise wing-like movements of their arms.
2. Divide the group into pairs. One person is a sculptor and the other person is clay. The sculptor shapes the clay into different positions, carefully moving the dancer into these positions. Change parts. Coach the sculptors to be careful in how they move the person who is the clay. The clay should be encouraged to follow the sculptor's lead. This is a good exercise to use for working on cooperative movement/behavior.

Making Connections

Talk about how we make/create things for the Sabbath and holidays. Have each participant share examples of things he/she makes. Some possible examples are: symbols, decorations, gifts. Discuss the importance of taking pride in the work.

Dance Midrash

Divide the group into trios. One person in each group is the carver and the other two will become the cherubim. The sculptor places the two cherubim in such a way as to interpret the phrase "turned toward the cover," and molds them into the desired shape. The sculptor is to create his/her human sculpture taking great care with detail. When the task is completed, the cherubim may "come to life," moving their upper bodies and arms, and conveying how they shield the cover. Change parts until everyone has had a chance to be the sculptor.

Challenge

Cherubim are also mentioned in Genesis 3:24. In this verse they are stationed east of the Garden of Eden to guard the way to the tree of life. Have participants create a dance in which they are cherubim protecting sacred places. It is believed that the cherub had the body of an animal such as a bull or lion and the head of a human. Encourage dancers to capture the uniqueness of these creatures. To enrich the improvisation, bring in appropriate pictures of Mesopotamian and Egyptian sculpture.

Exodus
Beginner ■ □ □

Colored Gate

And for the gate of the enclosure [of the Tabernacle], a screen of twenty cubits, of blue, purple, and crimson yarns, and fine twisted linen, done in embroidery. (Exodus 27:16)

Description

Instructions for the enclosure of the Tabernacle were given. The finished cover was to be richly colored and carefully embroidered.

Motivating Movement

1. Prepare ahead of time ten or so large cards, each a different color. Ask dancers to respond to each card with movements reflective of the moods and feelings aroused by the colors. Examples:
    a. Red - fiery, impassioned movement
    b. Blue - serene, steady movement
    c. Yellow - vibrant, "happy" movement

Making Connections

Ask participants what their favorite colors are and why. Have them describe various sanctuaries they have seen. If they were designing their ideal sanctuary, how would it look? Ask for the basis of their choices of color, design, and texture. If desired, have participants paint or make a three-dimensional model of their ideal sanctuary.

Dance Midrash

Divide the group into trios. Each dancer is to be a color—blue, purple, or crimson. In the improvisation dancers are to interact as if together they are weaving and embroidering the cover of the Tabernacle. Each dancer's movement should be based on moods and feelings aroused by his/her particular color.

Challenge

This improvisation is to take place on the pulpit. The dancers are divided so that a third are blue, a third are purple, and a third are crimson. They should be dressed in their color and/or holding yarn, scarves, or ribbon in their color. They choreograph a dance in which they create a human "fabric" to cover the ark. They should take inspiration not only from their individual colors, but also from the architecture of the sanctuary; the colors of stained glass, carpet, and/or painted walls; the textures and shapes of the objects on the pulpit.

Exodus
Intermediate ■ ■ ☐

Anointment

Take the anointing oil and pour it on his head and anoint him. (Exodus 29:7)

Description

In this verse God tells Moses how to consecrate Aaron as the High Priest.

Motivating Movement

1. Dancers imagine they are dirty and sweaty, and that there is a shower on the other side of the room. Individually, they move across the room in ways that reflect their feelings. When they reach the "shower," they imagine the water pouring over them, cleaning them. After their "showers," they return to the side of the room in which they began, moving in ways that reflect their new state of cleanliness.
2. Dancers imagine the room is gradually filling up with oil. They move around in the oil, exploring the "feel" of it as a slick film on the floor, a pool of oil, etc. The leader slowly calls out the level of the oil (a film on the floor, up to the ankles, to the knees, etc.).

Making Connections

Have dancers come up with examples of physical and ritual experiences which somehow change a person. In what ways does the person remain the same? In what ways is the person different? Examples of experiences include: showering, reaching the top of a mountain, taking an oath of office, converting to another religion, getting married, becoming a Bar or Bat Mitzvah or a Confirmand.

Dance Midrash

Divide the group into trios. One person is Aaron, another is Moses, and the third is the oil. The goal is for Moses to anoint Aaron with the oil. These are the expectations of the three participants:

    Moses is directive and official as he dances the process of anointing Aaron with the oil.

    The oil's movement is malleable and lithe as he/she is manipulated by Moses in order to carry out the ritual.

    Aaron is receptive and solemn.

When Aaron has been anointed, all three participants should move in ways that express how they are changed by this event.

Challenge

Have the dancers think of a time in their lives when a great change took place. What was the moment at which the impact of the change "sank in"? Have them improvise ways of ritualizing the change. Examples of pivotal moments representing a transition to a new state or experience:

    The moment of putting one hand on a Bible, raising the other, and taking an oath when being sworn into office

    The moment of breaking the glass at a wedding ceremony

    Signing the register of hikers who have made it to the top of a mountain

    The first time alone behind the wheel of a car

Exodus
Intermediate ■ ■ ☐

The Lure of Gold

> Aaron said to them, "Take off the gold rings that are on the ears of your wives, your sons, and your daughters and bring them to me." And all the people took off the gold rings that were in their ears and brought them to Aaron. (Exodus 32:2–3)
> Men and women, all whose hearts moved them, all who would make a wave-offering of gold to God, came bringing brooches, earrings, rings and pendants— gold objects of all kinds. (Exodus 35:22)

Description

In the first verse, the Israelites, discouraged by Moses' long absence on Mt. Sinai, decided to build a golden calf. Aaron told them to bring gold to be melted down to make the calf. In the second passage above, Moses told the Israelites that God had commanded them to bring gifts, including gold, to build the Tabernacle.

Motivating Movement

1. As a group, list adjectives which describe the precious metal, gold. Some examples are:
   Dazzling
   Brilliant
   Rich

Pretentious
Glittering
Gaudy

2. Write the adjectives on a card and have each person select one. If there are not enough cards to go around, have the group work in pairs sharing a card. The individual or pair improvises, depicting the adjective on the card.
3. Exchange cards. Repeat as many times as desired.

Making Connections

Discuss the positive and negative reactions we have to gold and wealth. Ask these questions: "Which public figures use their wealth in positive ways? In negative ways?" "On a personal level do you use material things in positive and/or negative ways?"

Dance Midrash

Divide the group in two. One half represents the community of Israel. As they bring their gold to build the golden calf, they are upset that Moses has been gone so long. The other half represents the community bringing gold to build the Tabernacle. Choose one spot in the room to which the gold is to be brought. Have both groups improvise at the same time, with everyone bringing the gold to the special spot while keeping in mind why they are bringing it—for the calf or for the Tabernacle.

Repeat a second time, reversing roles.

Discuss if their reason for bringing the gold made them feel or move differently. Repeat movements again, exaggerating these differences.

Challenge

In Exodus 32:3 the gold was brought to build an idol for the people to worship. In Exodus 35:22 the gold was to be used to build the Tabernacle. Have the group begin improvising the worshiping of a golden calf, with gold as the focus of their adoration. When that mood is totally established, call out "switch." Have the group imagine they are outside the Tabernacle which is also made of their gold, and of other beautiful materials. They are aware of God's presence in this very special place. Once this mood is well established, call "switch" again and return to the other mood. Repeat as desired.

Exodus
Beginner ■ □ □

Moses Sees the Golden Calf

> As soon as Moses came near the camp and saw the calf and the dancing, he became enraged; and he hurled the tablets from his hands and shattered them at the foot of the mountain.
> (Exodus 32:19)

Description

While Moses was on Mt. Sinai, the Israelites, discouraged by Moses' long absence, built a golden calf. They were dancing around it when Moses came down from the mountain. In his anger at seeing this, Moses threw the Tablets of the Law to the ground.

Motivating Movement

1. Have the group practice angry throwing gestures. Have them experiment with ways to expand the throwing gesture. Some examples are:
   a. Expand the gesture into a turn.
   b. Expand the gesture into a fall.
   c. Slow down the gesture.
   d. Stop the gesture in mid-action and then continue.
2. Teach the group a simple circle dance that could represent the dance the Israelites did around the golden calf. An example:
   8 skips going clockwise
   4 runs into center

4 runs back
8 skips counterclockwise
4 counts of spinning in place
Fall (carefully) to the knees
4 counts of bowing to the center

Dance Midrash

Create the scene described in the verse above. Have one person portray Moses while the others are the Israelites dancing around the golden calf. (You might have them use the dance taught in the "Motivating Movement" section above.) Encourage the Israelites to create a mood of adoration as they dance around the calf. Moses enters and sees the people dancing. Moses reacts by throwing the tablets to the ground. The Israelites respond to Moses' action.

Repeat several times, giving other participants a chance to portray Moses. These repetitions give the group several opportunities to establish more fully both the mood of adoration and their reaction to Moses' disapproval.

Making Connections

Have the group list examples and incidences of "golden calves" in today's society. Some examples might be: idolizing a rock star; placing too much importance on a material object, such as a mink coat or diamond necklace; or joining a religious group because of its beautiful building. Ask what impact these "idols" can have on their lives.

Challenge

1. According to a Midrash, when Moses threw the tablets to the ground, they shattered. However, the letters were not destroyed; they ascended to God. Have each member of the group chose a Hebrew letter. If it is a group that is just becoming familiar with the letters, you might bring in cards, each with a letter drawn on it. Each person is to portray the letter as it is ascending to God. A good resource book to get ideas about the letters is *Book of Letters* by Lawrence Kushner (New York: Harper and Row, 1975).
2. An advanced challenge. Read Exodus 32:1–6. Focus on the role Aaron played in making the golden calf. Divide the group into pairs. Have them create a duet between Moses and Aaron confronting each other as Moses sees the Israelites dancing around the calf. If the pairs wish, they may accompany their movement with appropriate words in English or Hebrew.

Exodus
Intermediate ■ ■ ☐

God Shields Moses

Station yourself on the rock, and as My Presence passes by, I will put you in a cleft of the rock and shield you with My hand until I have passed by. (Exodus 33:21–22)

Description

After the golden calf incident, Moses cried out to God, "Pray, let me know Your ways." After God's presence passed by him, Moses did what God asked him—he carved a second set of tablets.

Motivating Movement

1. Have dancers practice shielding movements. Coach them to use not only their hands and arms, but other parts of their bodies as well.
2. Have dancers stand in a circle and make shielding movements around one dancer who sits comfortably and quietly in the center. Everyone should have a chance to be in the center. Discuss the experiences of being a protector and being the recipient of protective energy.

Making Connections

Discuss with the dancers what they are most protective of and why. Also, ask them to describe both the feeling of being protected and their relationship to that source of protection. At what times do they sense they are moving amidst God's presence?

Dance Midrash

In the Bible, God is called by many names, including *"Tzur"* (Rock). God's name is "Rock," and Moses is shielded in the cleft of a rock.

Ask the dancers to imagine that the rock in which they are situated is actually the Rock that is God's presence itself. Have them move in the space as if it were suffused with God's presence, as well as God's protection.

Challenge

When Moses was in the cleft of the rock, he apparently witnessed something of God's presence that gave him the will to continue in his role as leader of the Israelites. What did Moses witness? In the improvisation the dancers are to dance the vision Moses witnessed. Possibilities include:

    The answer to the problem of good and evil

    The reason why God chose Moses to lead the Israelites

    A mystical reaching out to, or connecting with, Moses

    God's ultimate plan for the Jewish people through the centuries

Exodus
Beginner ■ □ □

Excellence for the Tabernacle

Moses then called Bezalel and Oholiab, and every skilled person whom the Lord had endowed with skill, everyone who excelled in ability, to undertake the task and carry it out. (Exodus 36:2)

Description

In the passage above, Moses identified who would be involved in the building of the Tabernacle.

Motivating Movement

1. Take one basic movement and teach it to the group, emphasizing the technique or skill needed to accomplish the movement correctly. Some examples of movements are:
    a. Grape vine step (used in folk dancing, in a circle counter clockwise, right step to the side, left foot crosses in front, right step to the side, left foot steps behind)
    b. Triplet pattern (used in modern dance, one low step followed by 2 high steps)

c. For those familiar with ballet—a basic step such as a pas de bourrée or glissade
2. Ask each person to demonstrate a single movement they do particularly well and teach it to the group.

Making Connections

Ask the group to think about what it means to have "talent" in a particular area. Is a person born with it? Is it acquired? What responsibility does "talent" carry with it?

Dance Midrash

Ask one person to portray Moses as he acknowledges those members of the community who have the skills necessary to build the Tabernacle. The others are the skilled craftspeople. They improvise movements which show the craft at which they are proficient. Some crafts are: wood carving, embroidering, skin tanning, working with precious stones, gold or silver smithing, weaving, etc. As they portray their various skills, Moses admires their work. As the improvisation continues, some of the craftspeople can work together. For example, the weaver provides the material for the embroiderer who is making the curtains for the altar that the wood carver is making.

Challenge

It has been said that while an artist is not a special kind of person, every person is a special kind of artist. Many of us have some "hidden" talent or skill. Perhaps we are embarrassed or insecure about letting others know about it. In this improvisation each person is to create movement which reveals a hidden talent. Each person is to imagine that this talent is needed by the community just as Bezalel's was, and that he/she is making an important contribution to the community by now using this previously "hidden" talent.

Exodus
Intermediate ■ ■ □

Levels of Sacred Space

> He placed the laver between the Tent of Meeting and the altar, and put water in it for washing. From it Moses and Aaron and his sons washed their hands and feet; they washed when they entered the Tent of Meeting and when they approached the altar.
> (Exodus 40:30–32)

Description

As the Tabernacle was completed, a laver, a vessel for washing, was placed between the Tent of Meeting and the altar. This enabled Moses, Aaron, and his sons to wash their hands and feet when entering the Tent of Meeting, and again when approaching the altar.

Motivating Movement

1. Divide the working space into three areas. Area one is for movements related to daily tasks. Area two is for movements related to special activities. Area three is for movements related to very special activities. Ask the group to move through all the defined spaces doing the kinds of movements appropriate to each space.

Dance Midrash

Redefine the three spaces used in the "Motivating Movement" section above. Now, area one represents the space just outside the Tent of Meeting, area two is the Tent of Meeting, and area three is the altar. The participants are Moses or Aaron as they move in the three spaces. They are to choose some kind of ritual movement to symbolize washing hands and feet before they move into area two or area three. Encourage them not to pantomime washing their hands and feet, but instead to find a ritual movement of preparation. Make the point that even the area around the Tent is sacred. They are entering three levels of sacred space with a repeated ritual of preparation.

Making Connections

Ask the group to talk about how they feel when they are called upon to perform a ritual act in the congregation (reading part of the service, lighting candles, reciting a blessing, etc.). Ask them to describe the first time they performed such an act or ask them to describe how they felt when they first entered religious school. Also, talk about ways the architecture of the worship place enhances "sacred" feelings.

Challenge

1. In the sanctuary repeat the Dance Midrash outlined above. Change the three areas as follows: area one is the place where the congregation sits, area two is the *bimah*, and area three is the space closest to the Ark. Remind the group to do ritual movements between the areas. What effect did moving in the sanctuary have on their movements?
2. Alternate idea: It if is not possible to dance in the sanctuary, visit the sanctuary as a group, perhaps with the Rabbi. What does the Rabbi feel when opening the Ark? How does the Rabbi feel when doing special rituals in specific spaces? Ask if the Rabbi does any particular preparation ritual before entering the sanctuary. After the visit, go back to the dance space and do the Dance Midrash again, applying any new insights.

Exodus
Beginner ■ □ □

The Cloud and God's Presence

The cloud covered the Tent of Meeting, and the Presence of God filled the Tabernacle. Moses could not enter the Tent of Meeting. (Exodus 40:34–35)

Description

Exodus concludes with Moses guiding the Israelites in the building of the Tabernacle. The verse above refers to God's acknowledgment of the Tabernacle's completion and God's promise to dwell amidst the Israelites.

Motivating Movement

1. Define the center of the room as a space which cannot be entered, but is the focus of the movement. As the group moves, it should relate to the center, perhaps by going around it. The center is always kept as the focus, but is never entered.

Dance Midrash

Have the group dance the reaction of Moses as he sees the cloud covering the Tent of Meeting and senses God's presence filling the Tabernacle. Although he knows he cannot enter, his focus stays on the Tabernacle. Coach the group to explore Moses' reaction as he watches the cloud cover the space. Some of his possible reactions are:

He prays, thanking God for keeping God's promise.

He calls the others to observe what is happening and to pray with him.

He reminds the Israelites not to abandon their faith as they did when they built the golden calf.

Making Connections

Ask the group to recall a time when an area has been defined as "off limits" to them. Did that area hold any special kind of fascination for them? Examples might be a police barricade or an area in their house which their parents asked them not to go into. How did they react to the limitation? Were they respectful of it, or did they try to sneak into the area when no one was looking?

Challenge

Moses did not enter the Tabernacle when the cloud filled the space. In contrast, two of Aaron's sons were consumed by fire when they violated the space (see Leviticus 10:1–3). Create an improvisation which contrasts the respect Moses demonstrated with the boldness and disregard that Aaron's sons must have exhibited.

Leviticus

Leviticus
Advanced ■ ■ ■

An Offering By Fire

> *The priest shall tear it open by its wings, without severing it, and turn it into smoke on the altar . . . it is a burnt offering, an offering by fire, of pleasing odor to the Lord.* (Leviticus 1:17)

Description

The verse above describes the last procedure in preparing a burnt offering of birds, turtledoves, or pigeons.

Motivating Movement

1. Bring an old newspaper to the session and hand each participant one sheet. Have them tear the sheet very slowly, being conscious of every aspect of the tearing, the energy required, the line of the tear, the changing of one shape to two shapes, the position of the arms as they move, the position of the body, etc.
2. Have the dancers imagine that each has been given a king-sized bed sheet. Again they are to make tearing movements, but this time they exaggerate their movement, using more of their bodies and intensifying their concentration.
3. Have the group improvise on odors. For example, the leader calls out an odor (rose, lemon, campfire, mothball, etc.) and the dancers move briefly in reaction to the odor.

Dance Midrash

The dancers are all priests. The improvisation is in three stages:

Each priest imagines holding a bird that is to be sacrificed. They dance with the "bird," exploring the heightened feelings the priest might have had as he was getting ready to prepare the bird.

They do careful tearing movements suggestive of the "tearing but not severing" of the bird.

They imagine they are watching the bird turn to smoke on the altar, and express their reactions in movement.

Making Connections

Have the group come up with examples of when it is necessary to take a position or an action that is less than the ideal. The position or action is a step in the right direction, but still a compromise in terms of the eventual goal. How should the decision to compromise be made? Some examples are:

Allowing sacrifice with strict rules when the ideal is worship in words and righteous action.

Having peacekeeping forces maintain the terms of a peace treaty between two countries. The ideal would be trust without the need of any military force.

Giving drug addicts clean needles so that contagious fatal diseases don't spread amongst them. The ideal would be no drug addictions.

Organizing shelters for the homeless. The ideal would be the building of permanent housing.

Challenge

Have dancers improvise more extensively as they respond to the imagined scent of the "pleasing odor to the Lord." Expand the improvisation to smells that are part of modern worship services. Some examples are:

The aroma inside a Sukkah

Incense used as part of a church service

Spices that are a part of the Havdalah service

Leviticus
Intermediate ■ ■ □

Drawing Near

When a person presents an offering. (Leviticus 2:1)

Description

The verse above appears before each of the many types of sacrifices that were mentioned in the Book of Leviticus. In Hebrew, the word for sacrifice or offering is *korban*, which also means "to be near" or "to draw near."

Motivating Movement

1. Designate a special place such as the center of a large circle or one far end of the room. Have dancers go as far from the place as possible. They are to pretend they are magnets slowly being drawn to the designated spot. Have them practice this in different tempos, particularly very slowly and very quickly.
    a. In a small group all may participate in the improvisation at once.
    b. In a large group or as an alternate experience for a small group, have each person be drawn to the designated spot. As another person begins to be drawn toward that spot, the first person is drawn back to the original starting place.

2. As a group, choreograph a way of approaching a designated spot. Much attention should be given to detail. Ask one person to set the kind of walk, another to determine the carriage of the arm, a third how the head is held, and so on. Have the whole group master the movement. Coach dancers to do the choreographed movement exactly as they created it.

Dance Midrash

Combine the idea of "drawing near" with the idea of giving an "offering" when the designated spot is reached. Also, experiment with the intent of the movement (hesitantly, enthusiastically, thankfully, or quickly to get it over with).

Making Connections

Discuss the idea that biblical sacrifice has been replaced in our Jewish worship today with spoken prayer. Apply the sacrifice movements explored previously in the "Motivating Movement" and "Dance Midrash" sections above to a personal prayer which might be uttered during the silent meditation. Ask each participant to improvise his/her own dance prayer using movement images of "drawing near." In this case, the dancers are not drawing near to a particular physical spot in the room, but perhaps to some kind of internal feeling. Just as in a service, close the improvisation of the personal silent prayer by singing and dancing together "May the Words of My Mouth," "*Shalom Rav,*" or "*Oseh Shalom.*"

Challenge

Specific types of sacrifices are discussed in Leviticus: the sacrifice of well being (3:1ff.), the sin offering (4:1ff.), and the guilt offering (5:1ff.). How might the motivation for the offering influence the way in which one "draws near"? Ask dancers when they would feel most compelled to draw close to God (during a time of grief, fear, guilt, celebration, thankfulness). As they dance have them infuse their movement with the emotion(s) appropriate to the reason for "drawing near."

Leviticus
Advanced ■ ■ ■

Holy on Contact

Anything that touches these shall become holy. (Leviticus 6:11)

Description

The verse above refers to the meal offering, the sin offering, and the penalty offering. Only Aaron and his descendants, the priestly line, were to eat of these offerings. If another sacrifice were to come into contact with these offerings, it also would become holy and only the priests could eat of it. Thus, holiness could be transmitted by means of contact.

Motivating Movement

1. Have the group stand in a circle holding hands. One person begins by creating a movement that ends with an arm tug or squeeze and passes it to the person next to him/her. The movement might be a kick, swing of the hips, and gentle push of the arm toward the next person. That person in turn passes on the movement to the next person, and so on until the movement has been passed around the circle several times.
2. The above is repeated. This time the person who begins the movement adds a quality of emotion to it, such as consolation, anger, affection. After the movement has gone around the circle, ask the dancers what emotional

intent they experienced through the movement. Repeat with different people initiating a movement.

Making Connections

Talk about traditions surrounding the ritual of reading the Torah in which holiness is somehow transmitted. Follow this with movement:

Dancers touch the Torah with a *tallit* or a prayerbook, and then bring the object to the lips. This is a symbolic gesture of bringing the words of Torah to our lips, that we might speak in ways that reflect Torah's wisdom. Repeat the gesture without using the actual objects.

Dancers pass the Torah as if from grandparent to parent to Bar/Bat Mitzvah. This is symbolic of the transmission of the Torah and its holiness from generation to generation. Repeat the gesture without using the Torah itself.

Ask the group to come up with any other examples in which holiness is transmitted.

Dance Midrash

Divide dancers into 3 groups: one is flour, a second is oil, and a third is Aaron and descendants.

Flour and oil:

Move in whatever ways capture their essences

Are gathered by Aaron and his descendants for the purpose of being offered on the altar

Are "turned to smoke" as Aaron and his descendants observe

Express their new essence—holiness

Aaron and his descendants:

Aaron and his descendants reverently shape the oil and flour into unleavened cakes. (These are the cakes from which only Aaron and his descendants could eat, and anything that touched these became holy.)

Dancers end by moving in ways which reflect the astounding experience of actually having created something holy. These movements would likely express fear, veneration, and exultation.

Challenge

The object is to transmit holiness through movement and touch. Divide the group into pairs. The task of the first person is to lead the second person to holy movement. The second person begins in a comfortable position while the first person shapes, transforms, and leads the neutral subject to elevated and holy movement. At the climax of the improvisation, both persons should be moving in ways that express the holiness initiated by the first person. Switch roles and repeat.

Leviticus
Intermediate ■ ■ □

Blood Ritual

Moses took some of its blood and put it on the ridge of Aaron's right ear, and on the thumb of his right hand, and on the big toe of his right foot. (Leviticus 8:23)

Description

A ram of ordination was slaughtered, and Moses used its blood as part of the ritual of ordination of Aaron and his sons as priests.

Motivating Movement

1. Have the group alternate between exploring isolated body movements and movements of the whole body. For example:
   Begin by moving the right hand only.
   Move the whole body.
   Move the left foot only.
   Move the whole body.
   Move the head.
   Move the whole body.
2. Have participants explore movement where the impetus comes from a specific part of the body and then spreads to the whole body. Some examples are:

   a. The left hand and arm lead into a series of turns to the left.
   b. The head leads in a forward/downward curve and back up again. This movement might be expanded into a forward somersault.
   c. The right foot slowly inches forward initiating a walk.
3. Have each person develop a movement phrase which follows the sequential pattern of touching his/her ear, thumb, and toe. Repeat the pattern several times.

Dance Midrash

Divide into pairs. One person is Moses and the other is Aaron. They are to dance the blood ritual, expanding the gestures into dance phrases in the following sequence.

   Moses dips his hand into imaginary blood, building a movement phrase that ends with touching Aaron's ear.

   Aaron responds to the touch, with his head initiating a movement phrase.

   Moses dips his hand in the imaginary blood, dancing a phrase that ends with touching Aaron's thumb.

   Aaron responds, initiating the movement phrase from his hand.

   Moses dips his hand in the imaginary blood, dancing a phrase that ends with touching Aaron's toe.

   Aaron responds, initiating the movement phrase from his foot.

Repeat, changing roles.

Making Connections

Lead a discussion on how "blood" is central to the ritual in the verse above. Some discussion questions:

   What might be the symbolic meaning behind the use of blood?

   What kind of emotional reaction do we have to using blood in a ceremony?

Challenge

The ritualistic action in this verse encompasses the whole body from head to toe. Have each person improvise a solo which incorporates the gesture of touching his/her ear (symbolic of purity of word), thumb (symbolic of action), and toe (symbolic of a righteous "path"), as a means of striving for purity of word and action.

Leviticus
Beginner ■ □ □

They Saw and Shouted

> And all the people saw, and shouted, and fell on their faces.
> (Leviticus 9:24)

Description

As part of the dedication of the Tabernacle, Moses and Aaron came out of the Tent of Meeting and blessed the people. Immediately following this, as a sign of God's presence, fire consumed the offerings on the altar. The people saw this and shouted.

Motivating Movement

1. Have the group make the following sounds, then make the sound with movement, and finally do the movement without the sound:
   Whispering
   Humming
   Shouting
   Screaming

Dance Midrash

Have the group be the Israelites who saw and shouted as the flames consumed the offering. As they see the sign of God's presence, they react by shouting. Ask the group to expand on the emotion that is being captured by dancing to shouting sounds. Some possible emotions are: awe, surprise, fear, disbelief, praise.

Making Connections

The Israelites are reacting to seeing "God's presence" during the dedication ceremony of a sacred place they helped build. Ask the group to share experiences they have had at a dedication ceremony (when a *mezuzzah* was affixed to a new home, the first service in a new sanctuary). What emotions did they experience? How did they express their feelings?

Challenge

There are three very different actions described in the verse: seeing, shouting, and falling. Have each participant create a dance which contains the following:

- 8 counts of small forward gestures representing seeing
- 8 counts of bold jumping movement representing shouting
- 8 counts of a sustained fall representing "falling on their faces"

Select one portrayal and have the whole group master it. Once everyone has learned the movement and the counts, have them perform the movement phrase in two different ways: all together and in several small groups "canon style," each group starting 4 counts after the preceding group.

Discuss the different emotional effect of doing the movement together as contrasted with doing it one after another, canon style.

Leviticus
Advanced ■ ■ ■

Unclean! Unclean!

He shall cover over his upper lip; and he shall call out, "Unclean! Unclean!" (Leviticus 13:45)

Description

In this section of Leviticus, we find described a variety of skin ailments (sometimes referred to as leprosy), and the ways the priest interacted with a person who had a skin ailment. The priest examined the ailment and then pronounced the person either clean or unclean. If a person was pronounced unclean, he/she called out "unclean" and separated himself/herself from the community.

Motivating Movement

1. Have the group make a circle. Each person in the circle says "unclean" or the Hebrew *"tamay,"* and spontaneously does a movement. Go around the circle several times. Discuss the kinds of movements which are done.
2. Explore the movement quality which illustrates the word "unclean." Usually the movement quality will be contracted and withdrawn.
3. Using the circle formation, have one person at a time go into the center of the circle, proclaim in movement the word "unclean" at least five times, and then withdraw from the circle ending outside of the circle.

Dance Midrash

Have the group improvise on the different aspects of and reactions to being "unclean." Some examples are:
- Surprise at discovering they are unclean
- Disdain with themselves
- Feeling isolated and separated from the community
- Facing the community
- Publicly exclaiming "unclean"

Making Connections

Discuss the current AIDS crisis. How does this relate to the Torah portion? One of the ways that AIDS is diagnosed is by visible spots that occur all over the body. A father of a person with AIDS made the comment, "AIDS is so humiliating because it's so public."

Have the group create a dance based on the reactions a person with AIDS might have upon seeing the spots all over his or her body. Encourage the group to imagine how they themselves would feel about having AIDS. How would they feel about others who have AIDS? Improvise the roles of these people: the father who feels humiliated, a person repulsed by what he/she sees, and a person who accepts and remains close to the individual with AIDS.

Challenge

Leviticus 13:46 says that people pronounced unclean shall be so as long as the disease is upon them. Being unclean, they shall dwell apart, outside the camp. Develop a dance about this community that dwells apart. What is it like? How do people treat each other (more sensitively or less so, timidly, fearfully, compassionately)? Have the group dance this community as it works toward building an atmosphere of supportiveness and healing.

Leviticus
Intermediate ■ ■ ☐

Contaminated Fabric

> *When an eruptive affection occurs in a cloth of wool or linen fabric.* (Leviticus 13:47)

Description

If there was some sort of fungus or mildew in a garment, the priest was called to examine it. The garment was isolated for seven days, reexamined, and either burned, or washed and isolated again. After the seven days, if the affection remained, the garment was burned; if not, the affected part was torn off. If the eruption reappeared, the garment was burned; if not, the garment was washed again and declared clean.

In part, this process may reflect an importance attached to clothing. In a society in which clothing may have been scarce, people didn't simply throw away something which required much time and effort to create.

Motivating Movement

1. Give each dancer a piece of fabric to examine while moving. The movement should take its inspiration from the dancer's focus on and connection with the fabric.

2. In the center of the space, set a pile of objects such as books, boxes, or clothing. Have dancers move the objects to the edges of the space in the following ways:
   a. With care and intent
   b. Carelessly and thoughtlessly

Making Connections

Discuss disposable items which we use in our everyday life, items which were not even available in ancient times. Examples are fast food packaging, pens, shavers, napkins, paper plates, plastic flatware, trash bags, newspapers. Because so much is disposable, how does this affect our attitudes toward the environment and toward our belongings? Ask the group what they would do if they found some sort of mildew or fungus growing in a piece of their clothing. How would their response to the mildew or fungus differ from the response of someone in the biblical world? What values would the different responses reflect?

Dance Midrash

The dancers imagine they are discovering in an article of clothing "an eruptive affection," a mildew or fungus. Each dancer decides whether to dance out his/her reactions to this eruption as a biblical or as a modern person. The group's improvisation will reflect two time periods simultaneously. Though dancers will be reflecting different time periods, coach them to react to, and interact with, each other.

Challenge

One person stands in the center of the space. Other dancers surround that person to form a physical "cloth" around him/her. The one dancer moves as if discovering an "eruption" in the human "cloth." The "cloth" and the dancer interact in movement. The dancer may express examining, isolating, washing, burning, or declaring clean. The (human) "cloth" may express both the passive roles of being examined, isolated, washed, burnt, or declared clean, as well as the active role of erupting an affection and either spreading or diminishing the affection.

Leviticus
Advanced ■ ■ ■

A Plague in the House

> *If when [the priest] examines the plague, the plague in the walls of the house is found to consist of greenish or reddish streaks, which appear to go deep into the wall, the priest shall come out of the house to the entrance of the house, and close up the house for seven days.* (Leviticus 14:37–38)

Description

The "plague" in the verse above was perhaps some sort of fungus growth. If the plague were to continue to spread, the house would have to have stones removed, then be scraped and replastered. If these measures had no effect, the house would have to be torn down. If, however, the plague did not spread, the priest would pronounce the house clean and carry out the appropriate ritual.

Motivating Movement

1. Assign dancers or have them choose different kinds of dwelling places to explore through movement. Ask them to spend a few moments thinking about and improvising on their various spaces. Ideas for spaces are: haunted house, mansion, rustic cabin, tepee, igloo, and jail cell. Have each dancer move individually in front of the rest of the group, which tries to guess what space is being "described" through dance.

Making Connections

Discuss how spaces can take on different meanings. For example:
  A sanitized, empty hospital room/a hospital room to which you have been assigned because of a serious illness
  A messy kitchen and dining area/a dining area prepared for a holiday
  An attic in an office building/the attic where Anne Frank and her family hid during the Holocaust
  A small apartment with a newlywed couple/the same apartment with the couple and newborn twins

Ask the group to share times when "neutral" spaces have taken on a cramped or "infected" feeling.

Dance Midrash

The dancers begin by forming into a square. They are to imagine that they are the walls of a house. They start out as normal, clean walls and slowly become infected with the plague. The plague might begin with one or two wall segments and spread to the others until the whole "house" has become infected. As the improvisation continues, dancers are sensitive to the energy and direction of the group concerning whether the plagued house will return to cleanliness or be demolished.

Challenge

Hang butcher paper around the walls of a room or a closed-off section of a room. Dancers move according to the mood which they feel the space conveys. After this mood has been established, place several jars of finger-paint (green, red, red-brown) in the center of the room. Dancers improvise movement as they paint/"infect" the walls with the colored plague. As they are painting and when they finish, they continue to be aware of moving according to new moods the space conveys.

Adding musical accompaniment to this improvisation may enhance the experience. Begin with harmonic sounds and move toward more dissonant sounds. Alternatively, the dancers can accompany this piece themselves with their voices and/or instruments.

This challenge can be repeated using different colors and the intention to paint something other than a plague. For example, bright, cheerful colors and the accompanying movements can be used to create a room of joy.

Leviticus
Intemediate ■ ■ ☐

Scapegoat

> Aaron shall lay both his hands upon the head of the live goat and
> confess over it all the iniquities and transgressions of
> the Israelites. (Leviticus 16:21)

Description

The verse above describes what Aaron, the High Priest of Israel, was to do on Yom Kippur. After Aaron confessed the iniquities, a goat (scapegoat) was sent off into the wilderness by a designated member of the community.

Motivating Movement

1. Have the participants pretend they are goats moving freely, grazing, or running on a mountainside. Build the dance improvisation based on the characteristic way a goat moves (e.g., butting with its head, pawing the ground, shaking away a fly, or scampering as if along a narrow mountain path).
2. Have each person begin by standing upright and tall, using his/her very best posture. Everyone imagines that heavy weights slowly are being put on their heads and shoulders. They move in response to the weights. The weights increase until the dancers can barely stand up or move. Reverse the process with the weights becoming lighter, so that the dancers can move again, and return to standing upright and tall.

Dance Midrash

Divide the group into pairs. One person is Aaron and the other is the goat. Without being literal, Aaron dances the confession of the "iniquities and transgressions of the Israelites," occasionally using the gesture of placing hands on the head of the other person. The other person, in a goatlike manner, responds by accepting the burden of the Israelites' iniquities. Repeat, changing parts.

Making Connections

Look at the traditional prayers in the Yom Kippur service. Ask questions such as: "Which modern-day rituals replace the ancient ones that Aaron performed?" Some examples are: reciting the *"Ve'al Ku'lam"* prayer, fasting, and prostrating oneself before the Ark. What emotional effect do the current rituals of Yom Kippur have?

Challenge

A High Priest and a scapegoat are not a part of the Yom Kippur ritual of today. Instead, each individual asks forgiveness for his/her own sins. Not only is forgiveness asked of God, it is also required from a person whom we might have wronged. Have the group make a circle. One at a time, a person goes inside the circle and dances the act of asking forgiveness from those standing around the circle, and/or from God. The other people sing, using a Yom Kippur melody. Especially appropriate is the melody which accompanies these words:

Ve'al Ku'lam, Eloha selichot,
Selach lanu, mechal lanu, kaper lanu.
For all these sins, O God of mercy,
Forgive us, pardon us, grant us atonement.

When the dancer has finished asking forgiveness, he/she rejoins the circle and another person goes in. Continue until each person has experienced being in the center.

Before starting, let the group know that there will be no discussion and that they will not be asked to explain their dance interpretation. (It is all right if someone prefers not to enter the circle and participates only by singing with the group.)

Leviticus
Intermediate ■ ■ ☐

Defiling the Land

> So let not the land spew you out for defiling it, as it spewed out the nation that came before you. (Leviticus 18:28)

Description

The Israelites were told that if they defiled themselves by copying the pagan practices of Canaan and Egypt, they would be spewed or vomited out of the land. Prior to this dire threat of punishment, the laws and rules listed had to do with sex offenses (see Leviticus 18).

Motivating Movement

1. Call out the following words and have dancers capture in movement their spontaneous reactions: reject, eject, spew, banish, oust, throw out, remove, discharge.
2. Have dancers capture in movement reactions to these words: obedience, allegiance, law abiding, careful, discipline. Encourage symmetrical and well-defined movements. Ask dancers to work toward developing a uniform style as a group.

Making Connections

First, have dancers express rejection. Ask them to come up with appropriate images, such as logs falling on the shoulders, a scratching on the heart, a bowling ball in the pit of the stomach, etc. Second, ask them to imagine that they physically are "the land." As land, what response would they give if they were "disobeyed" by being polluted in some way? Would they quake, erupt, become parched, turn their waters into foam? What similarities are there between a person's experience of rejection and the land's response to disobedience?

Dance Midrash

Define a circle of land in which God's laws and rules are firmly established and followed (see diagram on the next page). Outside the circle is a "nowhere" place into which the dancers as Israelites will be spewed. Dancers improvise as if they are moving obediently throughout the circle of land. Every so often they imagine what it would be like to be spewed from the land. Instead of just imagining, however, they actually dance out this image of rejection. After they "experience" the imagined rejection (in the nowhere place), they continue following God's laws and rules in the circle of land. They may experience the imagined rejection several times during the course of the improvisation.

Challenge

In this improvisation, feelings of rejection are explored in depth. The whole improvisation is to happen in the so-called nowhere place referred to in the "Dance Midrash" section above. The dancers together are a nation which has been spewed from the land. How do they react to this tremendous rejection, both as individuals and as a community? They might keep in mind the way communities have responded to pollution disasters caused by human beings, such as oil spills and nuclear accidents. Sometimes the community draws closer together, but sometimes the worst in people comes out.

Leviticus
Beginner ■ □ □

Leave Some for the Poor

> When you reap the harvest of your land, you shall not reap all the way to the edges of your field, or gather the gleanings of your harvest. You shall not pick your vineyards bare, or gather the fallen fruit of your vineyard, you shall leave them for the poor and the stranger. (Leviticus 19:9–10)

Description

The verses above describe voluntary moral actions which lead to holiness. In this case, the farmer was asked to leave part of the harvest for the poor and the stranger.

Motivating Movement

1. Have the group explore movements related to planting and harvesting.
2. Ask the group to dance the following:
   a. Greed—coach quick grabbing and pulling movements, gestures which take everything in sight.
   b. Enthusiastic generosity—coach giving movements which continue until they weaken the giver.

Dance Midrash

The entire dancing space is the field. Half the participants are farmers and half are the poor or strangers. Ask the farmers to begin by improvising planting and tending the entire field. Make the point that an important part of the improvisation is for them to care for all of the field when planting, watering, and weeding, even the area to be left unharvested. When the planting and tending are completed and the farmers begin to harvest, the poor and the strangers enter the improvisation to harvest the area left for them. The poor and the strangers may choose to interact with the farmers, or they may wait until the farmers have left the dance space and then enter to harvest. Do the improvisation again, changing roles.

Making Connections

Ask the participants to identify what in their lives might be analogous to the farmer's field. Ask what they do to help the poor and the stranger.

Challenge

First, have everyone think of someone they know who is in need of such basics as food and shelter. In an urban environment, this might be a homeless person who, with all of his/her belongings, sits at a particular street corner each day. Have each dancer develop a dance portrait of this person. Include in the dances imagined reactions to:

   Being given food directly by someone else
   Finding food which has been left for them
   Being turned down after asking for food

Coach participants to put themselves in the place of someone in great need.

Leviticus
Intermediate ■ ■ ☐

Stumbling Blocks

You shall not place a stumbling block before the blind.
(Leviticus 19:14)

Description

The verse above contains one of the commandments included in the "Holiness Code" (Leviticus 19:1–20).

Motivating Movement

1. Designate an imaginary line that cuts across the floor. Have dancers begin in the space on one side of the line and take turns walking toward the line. As they come to the imaginary line, have them stumble, recover, and continue walking. Repeat, exploring different ways of stumbling.
2. Have dancers imagine they are going down a flight of stairs, but have miscalculated. They assume they are on flat ground when there is really one more step to go. Have them try to capture that sensation in their bodies. Repeat, imagining that there is one less step than is calculated. Now, try this exercise "going upstairs."

3. The dancers spread out in the space. Each draws around himself/herself an imaginary circle with a radius of about 3'. They close their eyes and move within their own space, paying attention to how it feels to move without seeing, while being aware of others in the room.

Dance Midrash

Designate part of the room in which, as the improvisation develops, an imaginary obstacle will be located. At first, the dancers are able to move throughout the whole space. As the improvisation continues, they are no longer able to move beyond the area designated as an obstacle. The dancers' movements become thwarted and they begin to stumble. The emotional quality of the movement goes from comfort to frustration to anxiety and fear.

Making Connections

Ask dancers to come up with metaphors for "stumbling blocks" and "the blind." Examples are: addictive drugs and those unaware of their effects, false and costly "cures" and the terminally ill, get-rich-quick schemes and victims of manipulation, cults and those who are pressured or misled into them.

Ask which contemporary advertisements the participants consider to be stumbling blocks of a sort.

Challenge

1. Read Leviticus 19:14: "You shall not insult the deaf, or place a stumbling block before the blind. You shall fear your God: I am the Lord." Fearing God should lead to holy behavior. Unholy behavior includes insulting the deaf and placing a stumbling block before the blind. (Other examples of unholy behavior can be found by reading Leviticus 19:1–20.) The dancers are to improvise on a specific unholy behavior of their choosing and explore ways to transform it into holy behavior. Repeat the improvisation exploring different unholy behaviors.
2. Have dancers repeat the "Dance Midrash" above, but this time have them imagine a protective barrier rather than an obstacle. Coach them to modify their movement based on this new image.

Leviticus
Intermediate ■ ■ □

Love the Stranger

The stranger who resides with you shall be to you as one of your citizens; you shall love the stranger as yourself, for you were strangers in the land of Egypt. (Leviticus 19:34)

Description

God commanded Moses to speak to the whole Israelite community and tell them to be holy. One of the ways the Israelites were to show holiness was to treat the stranger with the same love they accorded to their fellow citizens.

Motivating Movement

1. Play a recording of today's popular music. Ask dancers to improvise being at a party listening to the music, dancing, and having a good time with their friends.
2. Next play music from a different period, such as the Charleston from the 1920s. Ask dancers to improvise being at a party where they don't know anyone and don't know how to dance to the unfamiliar music. Ask them to show how they are feeling by reacting in movement.

Dance Midrash

Divide the group. One half is the strangers and the other the Israelites. Have the Israelites begin by clearly establishing that they are a community enjoying a celebration together. Small groups of strangers enter. The Israelites react to them, more or less acknowledging them, and sometimes including them in the celebration. The goal is to depict various ways of reacting to strangers that would be in keeping with the ideal of holiness. Repeat, changing roles.

Making Connections

Ask each person to describe a time when he or she felt like a stranger. What were his/her emotions and feelings? Were the emotions changed by his or her interactions with others?

Challenge

Focus on the phrase "You were strangers." Building on the discussion in the "Making Connections" section above, have each person create a solo about being a stranger. Coach dancers to create a short, very specific solo composition. Each person should take great care that each move and gesture contributes clearly to the topic and that there are no unnecessary movements. Share the dances with each other and give feedback. Which movements enhance the emotion and which are unnecessary and need to be edited out?

Take time for each person to rework the dance composition, making changes based on the feedback given by the group. Share the studies again with each other.

Leviticus
Advanced ■ ■ ■

Etrog, Palm, Myrtle, & Willow

> On the first day you shall take the product of the hadar trees, branches of palm trees, boughs of leafy trees, and willows of the brook, and you shall rejoice before the Lord your God seven days. (Leviticus 23:40)

Description

The verse above outlines symbols required for the observance of Sukkot. These four species later became more defined as an etrog (citron fruit), myrtle, willow, and palm. To this day these species are held together and used ritually as part of the celebration of Sukkot. Dwelling in booths is another ritual requirement for Sukkot to remind future generations of how the Israelites lived in booths when God brought them out of Egypt.

Motivating Movement

1. Ask dancers to improvise movement that is precise, but without any emotional expression. A good image to give is that of dancing robots. Coach them to move in all directions.

2. Ask dancers to remain in place and explore expressing emotions. Have them focus on originating the emotion from their "centers" or gut, allowing the emotion to reverberate in their chests, shoulders, and faces. Have dancers repeat this exercise several times using different emotions: anger, ecstasy, grief, and fear.
3. Ask dancers to begin again as "dancing robots." Very gradually, have them introduce into their movement a given emotion. Have them continue improvising until they feel that the movement and the emotion are fully integrated.

Making Connections

Share with the group the following Midrash:

> The four symbols of Sukkot symbolize Israel. Just as the fruit of the hadar tree has taste as well as fragrance, so Israel has people who possess learning and good deeds. Just as the palm branches have taste but no fragrance, so Israel has people who possess learning without good deeds. Just as the myrtle has fragrance but no taste, so Israel has people who do good deeds but have no learning. And just as the willow has no taste and no fragrance, so Israel has people who have neither learning nor good deeds. What then does God say? Let the four symbols be tied together; they will atone one for another. The strength of one will offset the weakness of the others.

Discuss the Midrash with the group. Ask them if it rings true. Is the ending of the Midrash a good solution?

Dance Midrash

Refer to the above Midrash. Assign each dancer to be one of the four types of people. For the improvisation, movement without expression will be symbolic of learning ("taste"), and emotion will be symbolic of good deeds ("fragrance"). The person who symbolizes no learning and no good deeds will begin motionless and expressionless. That person will begin to dance only as others encourage him/her to move and to be part of the community. The group is to improvise a dance in which the four types of people work to complement each other in order that they become "tied together" as a balanced community.

Challenge

Again, refer to the Midrash. This time, have every dancer think of a plant or a fruit which seems to capture the essence of who he/she is. Then have each dancer individually choreograph a short study which captures those qualities of the plant or fruit expressive of himself/herself. Coach the dancers to be as specific as possible about those qualities. Have dancers share their "autochoreographies" with each other.

Leviticus
Beginner ■ □ □

Sound the Shofar

A sacred occasion commemorated with loud blasts. (Leviticus 23:24)
Then you shall sound the horn loud. (Leviticus 25:9)

Description

These two verses reflect the importance of sounding the shofar. The first verse refers to the ushering in of the Day of Atonement (Yom Kippur), while the second verse refers to the announcing of the Jubilee Year.

Motivating Movement

1. Have someone who can sound the shofar join the session. Begin by listening to the sound of the shofar. Talk about and analyze the rhythm and tone pattern. Take just one of the shofar patterns and ask the group to put the sound into movement. Repeat that pattern several times. Do an echoing sequence in which the shofar is played and the dancers then capture the sound in movement. Repeat the process using the different traditional shofar sounds.

Making Connections

Talk about how music and sounds are used to capture attention or to bring people together as a group for a particular event. Some examples are: music at a political rally, the singing of "The Star-Spangled Banner" at a baseball game, and the playing of the shofar at the end of Yom Kippur. Discuss the impact of the sound on the event.

Dance Midrash

Have the group begin by dancing routine activities. When they hear the shofar, it attracts their attention. They stop their routine activities and come together as a group around the shofar player. They greet each other and circle around the shofar player as a unified group, following the rhythm and melody of the shofar sound. When the sound stops, the dancers stop, too. They hold their final position silently and attentively.

Challenge

Instruments are often mentioned in the Bible. Psalm 150 contains mention of instruments played to "praise God." Experiment with dance inspired by this Psalm. Some suggestions are:

> Have the group capture the different qualities of the instruments in the same manner as was done with the shofar sound in the "Motivating Movement" section above.

> Have the group move with actual instruments, playing as they move. This works particularly well with drums. Their voices, singing or chanting, can also be their accompaniment.

> Have the group experiment with sounds the body can make when moving, such as clapping, stomping, and tapping the hands on different parts of the body. (Note the different sounds made when tapping the hand on different parts of the body.)

Psalm 150 can easily be developed into a choreographed piece to share with other classes or groups. You might choose a musical setting of Psalm 150 to accompany the work, or chant the Psalm as you dance.

Leviticus
Intermediate ■ ■ □

The Jubilee Year

Proclaim release throughout the land for all its inhabitants.
(Leviticus 25:10)

Description

This is a verse about the Jubilee year. This 50th year begins with the sounding of the shofar on its Day of Atonement. The features of the Jubilee Year are: the land was to lie fallow, all property was to revert to its original tribal owners, and all Hebrew slaves were to be set free.

Motivating Movement

1. Have the group experiment with confining positions, as if the body is tied in knots. Have each person find a bound position on count 1, and hold it for the next 3 counts. Repeat this pattern until the group successfully portrays bound movement.
2. Using the same structure as above, portray the motion of "release" on count 1, and hold it for the next 3 counts. Repeat the pattern several times.
3. "Proclaim" is a strong word. Ask each person to be a leader who proclaims something of importance to the community. Create a dance which reflects the important news.

Dance Midrash

Divide the group into pairs. One person is a slave owner. The other person is bound as a slave (they may use the bound movement they explored earlier or a more subtle portrayal of being bound psychologically). The improvisation is to depict the owner freeing the slave and the slave acknowledging his/her release from slavery. Reverse roles and repeat the improvisation. Encourage the group to experience fully the emotions and reactions of each role. Does the relationship between the slave and the slave owner change by the end of the improvisation? Do they become equals?

Making Connections

Talk about experiences when we have freed an animal or a person that is caught, perhaps an animal caught in a fence. How does it feel to have released the animal from such a situation?

Also discuss the idea of finding oneself in a "bound position," perhaps of one's own doing. Examples: binding oneself to an idea and then experiencing release when one leaves that mode of thought; having too much work and needing to stay to finish it, but wanting to be somewhere else (when the work is finally finished, how does one feel?).

Conclude with a discussion of unequal relationships that change to equal ones. Some examples of this are siblings who in later years see each other as equals, a student/teacher relationship that becomes a friendship. How might the feelings in both phases of the relationship be the same? How might they be different?

Challenge

1. This verse is more universally translated, "Proclaim liberty throughout the land unto all the inhabitants thereof." Substituting liberty for release somewhat changes the meaning of the verse. Begin with a discussion of the difference between the words "release" and "liberty." (Note: The word "release" is an action word that implies movement or change, while the word "liberty" is a state of being.) Illustrate the difference in dance.
2. Ask the group to identify those around them who are not equal in our society (e.g., the homeless). How might a redistribution of property as required in the Jubilee Year impact on this problem? Create a dance which portrays a problem of social inequality and ways in which society might "release" itself from that social ill.

Leviticus
Intermediate ■ ■ □

Reward and Punishment

If you follow my laws and faithfully observe my commandments, I will grant your rains in their season, so that the earth shall yield its produce and the trees of the field their fruit. (Leviticus 26:3–4) *And if . . . you do not obey me . . . I will make your skies like iron and your earth like copper, so that your strength shall be spent to no purpose. Your land shall not yield its produce, nor shall the trees of the land yield their fruit.* (Leviticus 26:18–20)

Description
To obey God's commandments led to blessings; curses came to those who disobeyed. "Skies like iron" means hot and rainless days, and "earth like copper" means hard and unfertile soil. In the text the verse of blessing is followed by a list of other kinds of blessings, while the curse is followed by more curses. This section presents one biblical viewpoint concerning reward and punishment.

Motivating Movement
1. Everyone imagines that they are sprouts in the ground. Dancers use strong, steady types of movements as they grow into tall, fruit-bearing trees.
2. Everyone imagines they are tall, fruit-bearing trees. They are to weaken and slowly shrink and shrivel.
3. Everyone creates two eight-count phrases. In the first phrase they are the imagined recipients of a blessing, in the second, recipients of a curse.

Making Connections

Lead a discussion on reward and punishment. Ask to what extent the group believes in one of the following systems of reward and punishment:

On the divine level God rewards and punishes.

On the interpersonal level, if a person is kind or cruel to others, he/she will be "rewarded" or "punished" by means of how others will treat him/her in return.

On the individual level, if a person takes little care of himself/herself, that becomes a sort of self punishment. A person who takes good care of himself/herself leads a productive and healthy life.

Dance Midrash

Have half the group be a community that has been faithful to, and observant of, God's laws and commandments, and is enjoying the concomitant blessings. The other half has been unfaithful and disobedient, and is suffering from being punished. The group should focus on the blessing and curse presented in the verses above. After each subgroup establishes the sense of being a blessed or cursed community, the individuals from the two communities can interact. Possible experiences in the interaction might include:

The accursed being jealous or resentful of the blessed

The blessed acting self-righteously

The accursed showing regret or repentance

The accursed eager to emulate the blessed

The accursed purposefully ignoring the blessed and vice versa

Challenge

Read Leviticus 26. Have each individual choose a different curse or blessing to portray through dance. The result should be a dance "fabric" of woven curses and blessings.

Examples of God's blessings from Leviticus 26 include:

You will have your fill of bread.

You will become fertile and multiply.

There will be peace in the land and you will be untroubled by anyone.

The land will have respite from vicious beasts. God shall dwell among you.

Curses include:
　Your land shall not yield its produce.
　Wild beasts will be let loose against you.
　You will eat the flesh of your sons and daughters.
　Your cities will be laid in ruin.
　You will not be able to stand your ground before enemies.

Leviticus
Beginner ■ □ □

Clearing Out the Old

> You shall eat old grain long stored, and you shall have to clear out the old to make room for the new. (Leviticus 26:10)

Description

This is one of the blessings promised the Israelites if they faithfully observed God's commandments. This blessing of abundance is included in a list of many blessings. Following these blessings is a list of curses that will befall the people if they do not observe God's commandments.

Motivating Movement

1. Have the group imagine that there is an enormous hill of sand in the middle of the space. They are to "clear out" the sand using as many different kinds of clearing movements as possible (e.g., as if using shovels, buckets, pushing with hands and feet, etc.). Encourage dancers to exaggerate their movements, making them as large and full as possible.
2. Repeat the above. This time, however, half the group clears out the sand while the other half keeps adding to the hill.
3. Have the group improvise heaviness of the body and lightness.

Dance Midrash

"You shall eat old grain long stored" implies that even as new grain comes in, the old is consumed first. The old must be dealt with before the new can replace it.

Divide the group into pairs and have them do the following improvisation in turn: One person begins in the center and moves as if he/she is a massive and weighty mound of grain. The second dancer tries to "clear out" the first dancer, using a variety of appropriate movements. The first dancer, whose movements will begin heavy and become lighter, slowly allows himself/herself to be "removed" from the center of the space. After all pairs have improvised in front of the rest of the group, the pairs switch roles and repeat.

Making Connections

Have the group talk about garage sales (the decision to have one; preparing for one; the end result of having had one, i.e., old things gone, new things in their place, more space in the house, etc.). How does it feel to get rid of something and replace it with a new item?

Take the garage sale notion and make it personal. What old bad habits would the participants "clear out"? What new habits and attitudes would replace the old ones?

Challenge

Each dancer imagines that he or she is a house. In each room of the house is an old habit or attitude which the dancer wishes to get rid of. The dancers improvise solos in which they go through each "room," confronting the imagined old habit or attitude, and gradually "replacing" it with a new, improved one. After they complete the change in one "room," they go on to the next (up to six or so rooms).

Numbers

Numbers
Beginner ■ □ □

In the Wilderness

The Lord spoke to Moses in the wilderness at Sinai. (Numbers 1:1)

Description

The Book of Numbers opens with a reminder that the Israelites are in the wilderness of Sinai. God told Moses to take a census of the community.

Motivating Movement

1. Have the group become elements of nature in the Sinai wilderness:
   a. The sun causing extreme heat
   b. The whistling wind which sculpts the landscape
   c. The flash floods raging down canyons
   d. The numerous stars shining brightly in the seemingly endless night sky
2. The dancers pretend that they are hikers in the desert. Have them dance their reactions to the elements listed above.

Making Connections

Ask the group to share personal experiences of camping and hiking in a desert or wilderness area. Talk about how the rough environment contrasts with the conveniences of city living. Fantasize together what it must have been like to spend 40 years in the wilderness. Ask the question, "How did the wilderness experience affect the Israelites?"

Dance Midrash

The Torah is sometimes referred to as a tree of life, a source of light, a fountain of living water. These are especially appropriate metaphors, considering that the Torah was given to the Israelites in the wilderness. Have the group improvise embracing an imaginary Torah while living in the desert wilderness. The Torah represents the nurturing elements of the wilderness—a tree giving shade from the hot sun, or a light to find one's way at night, or water to slake one's thirst.

Challenge

In the first chapters of Numbers, Moses was commanded to take a census of the people who were to camp under the banners of their ancestral house around the Tent of Meeting.

Divide the participants into groups. Each group will represent one of the tribes and create a banner (see Genesis 49:3–27 for ideas). Using the banner as a prop, each group is to improvise a dance which reflects the images on their banner and is descriptive of surviving life in the wilderness.

To share the dances, begin by having the tribes sit around a central space that is symbolic of the Tent of Meeting. Each tribe displays its banner and in turn dances in the center space.

Numbers
Intermediate ■ ■ □

Blessing of Peace

The Lord bestow favor upon you and grant you peace.
(Numbers 6:26)

Description

The verse above is the last line of the Priestly Benediction which Aaron and his sons were to use in blessing the people of Israel. The blessing consists of three phrases: The Lord bless you and keep you; The Lord deal kindly and graciously with you; The Lord bestow favor upon you and grant you peace. This blessing is used today at the end of services, during the *Avot* prayer, on Sabbaths and special holidays, during certain life cycle events, and by parents in blessing children.

Motivating Movement

1. Have the group explore dissonant movement. Louis Horst and Caroll Russell describe such a movement as "tense, full of potential action, one part pulling against another. [A movement reflective of] a conscious search for the physical sensation, deep in the muscles, for the texture which speaks of a tension characteristic of the modern world" (*Modern*

Dance Forms in Relation to the Other Modern Arts, San Francisco: Impulse Publications, 1961, 50–51).
2. Once the dissonant movement is clearly realized, ask the group to explore the opposite kind of movement—fluid movement in which the body moves as a whole without tension. Remind the group that this doesn't mean lethargic movement. Explore purposeful movement without opposition.
3. Teach the traditional gesture which accompanies the blessing—lifting the hands and spreading the thumb and middle two fingers to create the Hebrew letter *Shin* (see illustration on the following page). (Note: The word for peace, *Shalom*, begins with the letter *Shin*.) Have the group improvise, using this gesture as the theme of their movement.

Dance Midrash

Ask participants to be Aaron or one of his sons. Moses, following God's instructions, has just given them the words of the blessing. (Since so much of their lives has been filled with strife, Aaron and Moses particularly want to find a way to convince the people of Israel that peace is possible.) Everyone is to portray Aaron blessing the people with the words in the verse above. Use movement which is not dissonant and represents a wholeness of purpose.

Making Connections

As a group, go through the prayers of a typical worship service and see how often the word "peace" occurs. Does peace always have the same meaning? Discuss both a personal feeling of peace and how one might strive to achieve it, then discuss world peace and how one might be active in promoting it.

Challenge

Have the group imagine they are on a world tour promoting peace. Together, choose three countries to visit. Create a dance for each country that incorporates the words of a message of peace relevant to the particular situation in the country. End each dance with the benediction, "May the Lord bestow favor upon you and grant you peace."

Numbers
Intermediate ■ ■ □

Shouldering the Sacred

> But to the Kohathites, [Moses] did not give any [carts and oxen]: since the [Kohathites'] service was that of the [most] sacred objects, their porterage was by shoulder. (Numbers 7:9)

Description

The chieftains of the tribes of Israel brought carts and oxen to Moses. Moses gave them to the Levitical families for use in moving the Tabernacle and its objects. However, Moses did not give any carts or oxen to the Kohathite family, since they were to carry the most sacred of objects on their shoulders.

Motivating Movement

1. Guide the dancers in exploring movements made with the shoulders:
    a. Circling the shoulders one at a time, both together, forward, and backward
    b. Moving up and down one at a time, both together, slowly, and quickly
    c. Shaking
2. Have the group experiment with dancing different ways of carrying things:
    a. Carrying a tiny object in the center of one hand using the other hand to shield it, and moving the body carefully so as not to jar or drop it

b. Carrying a very heavy pile of logs using hands and forearms
c. Carrying a basket of fruit on the head with the hands helping to hold it in place; balancing the same basket without the help of the hands
d. Carrying a child on the hip
e. Carrying a large object on the upper back and shoulders

Dance Midrash

Divide the group. Half portrays Kohathites carrying on their shoulders and upper backs large objects suspended from staves. Half portrays loading ox carts with objects from the Tabernacle. Begin the improvisation by dancing how the Kohathites pick up their sacred objects and put them on their shoulders while the others are loading carts. Then depict the journey. Coach the Kohathites to emphasize the special responsibility they have. They carry while others simply walk alongside the carts. The improvisation ends when the mood of the journey has been well established. Repeat, changing parts.

Making Connections

Ask the group what the phrase "shouldering responsibility" means, particularly as it relates to religion. Discuss its negative and positive connotations (e.g., charitable obligations that weigh one down versus pride in contributing despite the sacrifice).

Challenge

1. Improvise on the phrase "shouldering responsibility" from an abstract point of view. Coach the group to go first with the image of a heavy burden weighing them down. Switch to the image of bearing the heavy weight with pride. Conclude by exploring the dynamic of going from one image to the other.
2. The Torah is read from beginning to end each year. The completion is celebrated on Simchat Torah by carrying the Torah scrolls seven times around the sanctuary (*Hakafot*)—a modern-day example of carrying a sacred object. Have the group choreograph a dance of seven *Hakafot*. Each circling is to have a separate and distinct rhythm and quality reflective of ways of serving the community (e.g., giving of one's time or financial resources, determination to maintain ritual observance, joyful celebration of the holidays, welcoming the stranger, teaching traditions, studying, prayer).

Numbers
Intermediate ■ ■ □

The Wave

And let Aaron designate the Levites before the Lord as a wave offering from the Israelites, that they may perform the service of the Lord. (Numbers 8:11)

Description

The descendants of Levi, the third son of Jacob and Leah, became the priests of Israel. They were allowed access to the Tabernacle and to its sacred objects. In the verse above, no animal or grain was placed on the altar as an offering. Instead it was the actual movement made by the Levites that was the offering.

Motivating Movement

1. Pass around a conch shell. Have everyone listen to it with their eyes closed. Ask the participants to start in a kneeling position and to put the sound they have just heard into their bodies. Have them remain on their knees, encouraging them to see how many different ways they can create ripple or wave-like movement. Doris Humphrey, a pioneer modern dancer, created a very powerful dance based on wave images called "Water Study." A film of this dance may be obtained from Dance Film Archives, University of Rochester, Rochester NY 14627.

2. Progress to movement which covers space in a wave-like manner, going either forward and backward or side to side. Emphasize the swing-like rhythmic quality. If you choose to accompany the group with clapping, a drum, or music, 6/8 time works best for this type of movement.

Making Connections

Talk about ceremonies in which a person takes on a new role in his/her life. Some examples are: becoming ordained, getting Confirmed, getting married, or becoming a Bar/Bat Mitzvah. What kinds of emotions are experienced? Include these emotions when dancing the following Dance Midrash.

Dance Midrash

Begin by specifying one part of the room as the altar. This will be the place where the wave movement will reach its climax. Have the participants assemble 15–20 feet away from the altar area. One person is to be Aaron. Aaron begins a wave-like movement which ends by touching one of the participants. That person then builds from Aaron's movement energy into a wave movement which takes the person forward to the altar area. The person expands the wave offering and then returns to his/her starting position. Aaron now moves on to another person. This continues until everyone has had a chance to reach the altar area.

Challenge

As a group, choreograph a ritual wave dance during which each member plays a specific role. Two possibilities are:

> Move exactly together as if part of a giant wave. The movement should be simple with specific counts so that it can be done in unison.
>
> Develop a sequential wave-like pattern in which one person's movement leads into another's.

The goal here is for the group to move as an ensemble, building a unison wave offering which they create together and perform together.

Numbers
Intermediate ■ ■ □

Miriam Stricken

As the cloud withdrew from the tent, there was Miriam stricken with snow-white scales. (Numbers 12:10)

Description

Miriam and Aaron spoke against Moses because of the Cushite woman he had married. Furthermore, they said, "Has the Lord spoken only through Moses? Hasn't God spoken through us as well?" God heard them and appeared before them in a pillar of cloud, chastising them for their gossip.

Motivating Movement

1. Have dancers do short, quick, repetitive movements representative of gossiping. Dancers can respond to and play off of their fellow dancers' movements and noises.
2. Have dancers imagine they are looking out of the window of an airplane at the masses of clouds. Have them move in a smooth and billowy way as if they are part of those clouds.

Dance Midrash

Divide dancers into pairs. One will dance the role of Miriam, the other Aaron. Begin by having the pair dance easily and lightly in a "dialogue" characteristic of siblings. Allow the dancers to develop more serious overtones, less lightness, until the interchange between them is clearly ugly and derisive. When all the pairs have come to this point, the leader moves across the space, representing the pillar of cloud. Miriam responds as if she is seeing the snow-white scales cover her body. Aaron then responds (with remorse, regret, pity, shock, fear, etc.) to seeing his sister being attacked with this disease.

Making Connections

Participants recall a close relationship with a sibling or a dear friend. Have them think of a conversation about a third party which started off innocently enough, but became almost vicious at the end. What caused the transition between good-natured conversation and unkind, unnecessary gossip? What was the result of the gossip? Did they regret their behavior? Did the gossip get them into trouble?

Ask the group why they think gossip or slander is considered such an evil. (There is a Jewish teaching that gossip or slander is the greatest of all sins. Robbery, adultery, and even murder involve only two persons, while gossip or slander involves three.)

Challenge

Review Numbers 12:1–16. After Miriam was stricken with scales, she was shut out of the camp for seven days. Have half the group dance the role of Miriam during her seven-day seclusion. The other half of the group, dancing the role of Aaron, imagines that they go to visit Miriam outside the camp. How do they approach her? How do they interact with her? What response do they get from her?

After the improvisation, dancers evaluate what they experienced and what they perceived were the similarities and differences between the ways the dancers expressed their roles. Repeat the improvisation imagining that it is Moses who visits Miriam.

Numbers
Intermediate ■ ■ ☐

Fringed Reminder

That shall be your fringe; look at it and recall all the commandments of the Lord and observe them, so that you do not follow your heart and eyes in your lustful urge. (Numbers 15:39)

Description

God commanded Moses to instruct the Israelite people to make fringes (*tzitzit*) on the corners of their garments. These fringes were to remind them to observe all of God's commandments and to be holy to God.

Motivating Movement

1. Bring in several different objects (e.g., a *tallit*, a candle to light, a Torah cover, a flower or branch). Pass an object around; encourage the dancers to look it over carefully. Once everyone has had a chance to hold and inspect it, have them dance their reaction to it. Repeat with each of the different objects.
2. Have dancers explore movements done at the same time that are in opposition to each other. Examples are: reaching down with an arm while stretching up with a leg, pushing a hip out to the side while leaning the upper body in the opposite direction, pushing forward with the arms while pulling back from the hips.

Making Connections

Have the group share experiences in which they have felt tempted to do something they knew was wrong. Ask where the temptation comes from, and why it is hard to resist. How might they resist acting on the temptation? Examples of temptations include gossip, deception, selfishness, stinginess, cheating.

Dance Midrash

Each dancer is given a *tallit* or scarf. They dance the ritual in which they hold the fabric, look at it thoughtfully, and wrap it around their shoulders or waist. As they continue moving, tempting movements begin to "pull" at them. They use the fabric (or the fringes) in some way to remind them of God's commandment (e.g., they might take the fabric off, look at and touch it, move with it, and put it on again).

Challenge

In pairs, one dancer is the temptation, the other is the "reminder." (A specific temptation and reminder should be agreed upon in advance.) The dancers improvise movement expressing the tension between them. More experienced and mature dancers can be encouraged to make physical contact, exploring resistance experienced in the give and take of each other's weight.

Numbers
Intermediate ■ ■ ☐

Moses Hears and Falls

When Moses heard this, he fell on his face. (Numbers 16:4)

Description

In the wilderness, Korah gathered 250 men to revolt against Moses and Aaron. Korah accused Moses and Aaron of going too far in their leadership and claimed that the whole community was holy (not just Moses and Aaron). The rebels questioned why Moses and Aaron raised themselves above the congregation. Moses responded to this accusation by falling on his face.

Motivating Movement

1. Guide the group in practicing different kinds of falls. Some specific suggestions are: body falls forward, backward, sideways; falls of isolated body parts, such as letting just an arm fall; falling at different speeds; falls that reflect a variety of emotions, such as anger, grief, humility, humiliation; a desire to escape a situation; falling as part of prayer; and intentional falling versus collapsing.

Making Connections

Ask dancers to think of a time when they fell down. Did they trip purely by accident or were they not paying attention to where they were going because their mind was elsewhere? Did they purposely fall? Recalling how they felt when they fell, have them dance and experiment with their falls. What were their feelings when they were on the ground?

Dance Midrash

Ask each person to be Moses reacting to Korah's words by falling. Coach them to experience the fall several times. Have them ask themselves the following questions as they improvise the scene:

Does Moses fall in front of the 250 men, or before God, or before both?

Does he fall out of humiliation or humility or exasperation?

Is Moses upset or angry?

Could the fall be part of a prayer?

Expand the improvisation to include not only the fall, but Moses' reaction before and after the fall.

Challenge

Read Numbers 16 and 17 with close attention to verses 16:4, 16:22, and 17:10, all of which include the phrase, "They fell upon their faces." Discuss the context of each of these verses. Divide the group into three sections. Ask each section to portray the different emphases of the phrase, "They fell upon their faces." Encourage each group to find a way to dance the uniqueness and particular nuances of their verse. Have each group share their "fall" with the others.

Numbers
Beginner ■ □ □

Striking the Rock

And Moses raised his hand and struck the rock twice with his rod. Out came copious water, and the community and their beasts drank. (Numbers 20:11)

Description

The Israelites were without water in the wilderness and began complaining to Moses. Moses was told to order a rock to yield water before the eyes of the assembled people. Instead of ordering the rock, Moses struck it. For this he was punished. He would continue to lead the Israelites, but he would not be allowed to enter the Promised Land.

Motivating Movement

1. There are three types of movement in the verse above. Have the dancers explore them:

    Striking

    Rushing forth

    Drinking in

2. Have them choreograph the following pattern and share it with the rest of the group: strike, rush forth, drink in; strike, rush forth, drink in; strike, rush forth, drink in.

Making Connections

Ask dancers to imagine this scenario: You are feeling tremendous pressures and stress because of your job or school or because of social or personal reasons. On top of everything, suddenly another pressure is added (an extra assignment, a surprise in your personal life, the loss of something valuable, etc.). Although the new pressure may be relatively unimportant in the scheme of things, imagine yourself overreacting. How do you feel? Is there a desire to react physically (throw a tantrum, punch the wall, throw objects, tear up or break something, stomp, scream into a pillow, strike someone or something)?

Dance Midrash

One dancer is Moses and the rest are rebellious Israelites. Moses tries to dance the role of a strong leader, while the Israelites complain to him with taunting and "pressuring" movements. Moses, becoming angry and "stressed out," strikes the rock. The Israelites respond to the rush of water with greedy thirst as Moses responds to the punishment God decrees for him.

Challenge

It seems exceedingly harsh that Moses was forbidden to enter the Promised Land just because he struck a rock. What was he really being punished for? Some possibilities are:

Hubris

Disobedience

Inappropriate anger

Loss of faith and trust

Your own idea

Have dancers choose one of the possibilities listed and dance the role of Moses during the few minutes preceding his striking the rock.

Numbers
Intermediate ■ ■ □

Copper Serpent

> Moses made a copper serpent and mounted it on a standard, and when anyone was bitten by a serpent, that person would look at the copper serpent and recover. (Numbers 21:9)

Description

The Israelites complained to Moses about the conditions in the wilderness. In response to their negativity, God sent fiery serpents among them. The Israelites, realizing they had spoken against Moses and God, asked Moses to intercede for them with God. God told Moses what to do.

Motivating Movement

1. Ask dancers to think of something they find scary (spiders, darkness, snakes, dogs, aliens, quicksand, thunder, etc.). Have them improvise on their reactions to encountering that something.
2. Ask dancers again to think of that scary something. This time when they encounter it, it is behind glass bars or whatever else would ensure a completely "safe" encounter. Have them improvise on their reactions.
3. Have dancers be the scary something!

Making Connections

Discuss the following fears people have, and ask the group to come up with suggestions as to how people might deal with or get over them: spiders, darkness, strangers, other suggestions.

Once the Israelites were able to see in perspective what they feared and what was harming them (mounted on a standard), they were able to recover. Discuss. Note that the copper serpent has become a medical symbol. A question to pose: How much of healing is in human hands and how much is in the realm of the divine?

Dance Midrash

Have dancers imagine they are Israelites. They begin by moving as if fiery serpents among them have frightened them, bitten them, and left them hurting. Ask dancers to pay close attention to how they relate to the (imagined) serpents. Possibilities include fast hops and jumps, leaps, shuffles, turns toward each other, hiding movements. Now have them challenge their own fears by trying to get perspective on the serpents and "befriending" them. Whatever approach they choose should eventually lead them to dance movements signifying the reduction of their fears and recovery from the serpent bites.

Challenge

This improvisation will focus on the process of recovery. Dancers will go from movements that are broken, weak, and diseased to ones that are whole, strengthened, and healthy. They can repeat this process several times. It may be helpful to explore beforehand how the above-mentioned qualities can be incorporated and expressed in movement.

During the improvisation, attention should be given especially to the transitions between the two types of movement, that is, how does one move from sickness to recovery? In addition, have them be aware of each other and how they might interact as they dance.

Numbers
Intermediate ■ ■ □

Balaam Blesses

How fair are your tents, O Jacob, your dwelling places, O Israel.
(Numbers 24:5)

Description

Balak, King of the Moabites, disliked and feared the Israelites because there were so many of them. He wanted to be rid of them. He invited Balaam, a respected soothsayer, to come to curse the Israelites. The effect of Balaam's words were believed to be quite powerful. Balaam arrived at Balak's palace. Even though Balaam agreed to curse the Israelites, God intervened and caused him to bless them abundantly.

Motivating Movement

1. Begin by having the group find movements which portray a curse. Coach them to make aggressive, sharp, percussive, and staccato movements which emphasize straight lines. When this is mastered, have the group improvise blessing movements (curved arms over head reaching toward the congregation, etc.). Coach circling and enveloping movements that might also suggest blessing.

2. When the contrasting movements above are understood, divide the group. Each half lines up on opposite sides of the room. One person dances to the center of the room in a way that suggests a curse. A second person from the other side of the room responds by dancing to the center of the room with a blessing movement. Repeat this process until everyone has experienced both cursing and blessing movements.

Making Connections

Ask participants to improvise or discuss a difficult or frustrating time in their lives when they wanted to curse. Perhaps it was after a fight with their parents, or when they got caught doing something they weren't supposed to be doing, or following the death of a loved one. Experiment in dance, taking this desire to curse and turning it into a blessing. Coach the group to feel as if they want to curse first so that they can experience how much energy it takes to change the impulse to a blessing movement.

Dance Midrash

Have dancers imagine they are Balaam intending to deliver a curse. Begin with an entrance that shows this intent. Explore the moment when the intent to curse changes into a blessing. Possibilities for expanding on that moment are:

Depict a wrestling between the two styles of movement until the blessing movement dominates.

Suddenly have the curse turn into a blessing, which leaves Balaam surprised at the change that took place. Perhaps the blessing was automatic and only after it was done a few times did Balaam realize the change and dance the blessing with the appropriate emotion.

Challenge

Read Numbers 22:2–34. Ask the group to imagine they are one of the servants accompanying Balaam. Unbeknownst to Balaam they are really Israelites disguised as servants. After witnessing what happened on the journey to Balak's palace, they hastily slip away and return to the camp of the Israelites. Now have the Israelite "servants" create a dance explaining what they have seen and their reactions to it.

Numbers
Advanced ■ ■ ■

Flaunting Leads to Death

> Just then one of the Israelites came and brought a Midianite woman over to his companions, in the sight of Moses and of the whole Israelite community who were weeping at the entrance of the Tent of Meeting. (Numbers 25:6)

Description

The Israelite community camped at Shittim, close to the Promised Land. Members of the community behaved badly, becoming involved with women from Moab in idolatry and in immoral acts. Among them was Zimri, who openly disregarded the moral code and flaunted his behavior with Cozbi, a Midianite woman. Pinchas, in order to turn God's anger away from the people and end the plague, followed Zimri and Cozbi into a chamber and stabbed them.

Motivating Movement

1. Have the group practice bold movements, especially big, strong walks, runs and leaps.
2. Have the group use the various rhythms of sobbing and improvise a "weeping" dance.
3. Divide the group. One half is to practice movement that is ordinary and doesn't call attention to it, while the other half is to dance in an attention-getting manner.
4. With an adult group, improvise movement which has sexual overtones.

191

Dance Midrash

Select dancers to portray Zimri, Cozbi, and Pinchas. The rest of the group represents the Israelite community. The improvisation begins with the community, which includes Pinchas, portraying weeping about immoral behavior and the plague which is affecting them. Coach the dancers to interact, showing they are a community with common concerns. When this is well established, Zimri and Cozbi enter boldly. Their movement illustrates that they are behaving in a brazen, inappropriate way, different from the community. The community reacts to their behavior. Some of their reactions might include weeping harder, turning their backs, anger. Pinchas should stand out in his reaction, which would indicate that he will do something special. The improvisation ends when Zimri and Cozbi leave the scene followed by Pinchas. Repeat, changing roles.

Making Connections

Lead a discussion about how communities react to behavior which is considered immoral. Consider such general examples as the Amish shunning someone for becoming too worldly, yelling at someone dressed inappropriately in the ultra-Orthodox sections of Jerusalem, and bringing a lawsuit against someone for "indecency." Getting more specific, discuss ways the participants censor behavior that is not part of their code. Some examples are: censoring yourself by not talking to someone, censoring group inclusion by blackballing a person from membership in the group, and censoring society by trying to get a law passed that serves the moral purposes of a particular group.

Challenge

Develop duets in which one person represents immoral and idolatrous behavior, and the other the accepted community norm. Let each pair evolve their own scenario. Some options are:

Idolatrous and immoral behavior wins out over the community norm. (Note: Is this a quick or a gradual process?)

The community norm wins out over the immoral behavior.

The two conflicting behaviors are in constant conflict with each other, both attempting to convince the other to change, but neither winning.

The two conflicting behaviors coexist side by side.

Numbers
Intermediate ■ ■ □

Daughters of Zelophehad

> *And the daughters of Zelophehad . . . came forward.*
> (Numbers 27:1)

Description

A census was taken by Moses and by Aaron's son Eleazar, and allotments of land were made as a result. Thus far only sons had inherited the property of their fathers. The five daughters of Zelophehad asked for equal treatment for their families since their father had died in the wilderness leaving no sons. The daughters asked that they be given a land holding. Moses brought their case before God. God, responding to their plea, told Moses to transfer their father's share to them.

Motivating Movement

1. Have the group practice making forward movements which command attention.
2. Have the group establish a basic movement, such as sliding from side to side or swaying. The group then does the movement together. Once the movement is established, a member of the group spontaneously does a new movement in a bold manner, going against the original movement. Members of the group now have the option of joining the new movement

or staying with the original. Repeat this until everyone in the group has had a chance to initiate a new movement. Discuss what it takes to get the group to go with a new movement.

Dance Midrash

Have a quintet portray the five daughters and develop a way to plead their case. Since each of the names of the daughters is given in the Bible, each may have had a distinct role in presenting her request. Encourage each quintet to move together in order to feel the momentum of a simple movement done as an ensemble. Alternate with one of the daughters leading a phrase while the others are doing supportive or related movements.

Making Connections

Say to the participants: "You're sitting amongst peers who are exchanging racist, anti-Semitic, or sexist jokes. You feel the jokes are insensitive and unfair. At what point will you feel compelled to speak up?" Ask them to identify that moment of transition from passive listening to speaking out for justice. Have them bring that intensity of emotion into the Dance Midrash improvisation as they do it again.

Challenge

1. Talk about today's social issues. Consider particularly groups which are not being treated equally and/or are requesting changes in the law. How are they making the request—proposal, demonstration, strike, etc.? Develop an improvisation keying in on a specific incident.
2. Using the song "We Shall Overcome," create a group dance which illustrates the positive energy of "coming forward" to initiate change.

Numbers
Beginner ■ □ □

New Moons

On your new moons you shall present a burnt offering to the Lord: two bulls of the herd, one ram, and seven yearling lambs without blemish. (Numbers 28:11)

Description

In the verse above, the types of sacrifices required for various sacred occasions are delineated. On new moons meal offerings, libations, and a sin offering were required in addition to the burnt offering. The celebration of the new moon was important in ancient days, especially as a women's holiday. Special prayers and readings are included for the new moon in synagogues today. Some women are trying to "reclaim" this new moon celebration (Rosh Chodesh) by creating new religious rituals sensitive to their life experiences.

Motivating Movement

1. Have dancers trace imaginary moon shapes with their fingers. Continue by asking them to trace these shapes with various parts of their bodies: elbows, shoulders, hips, knees, feet, head, etc.
2. Ask dancers to discover all the different types of moon shapes they can make with their bodies—explore half circles, crescents, and arcs.
3. Have dancers move across the space along moon-shaped floor patterns while making different moon shapes with their bodies.

Dance Midrash

Designate an area in the center of the space as the place where offerings are brought. Have dancers begin by standing in a circle around the central place. Have each dancer in turn improvise the giving of an imaginary offering. The improvised phrase of movement should use only moon shapes and moon floor patterns.

Repeat the improvisation with dancers giving their imaginary offerings at the same time. Encourage dancers to interact with each other, especially in terms of creating new and more expansive moon images.

Making Connections

Ask participants to share the most unusual or spectacular viewing of the moon they have witnessed (perhaps a moonrise, a moon viewed from an airplane, a moon like a great ball of orange fire, a crescent moon appearing in the daylight). Why and in what ways did this viewing stand out to them? Ask them to come up with songs, poems, stories, rituals, and religious myths inspired by the moon. Why do they think the moon elicits such feelings of awe and so much creativity?

Challenge

Have dancers choreograph a moon dance for Rosh Chodesh (the celebration of the new month) which includes glimpses of the moon at all the various stages of its approximately 29-day cycle. Coach dancers to capture what is spiritually inspiring and aesthetically pleasing about the moon. Optional thematic undercurrents to be explored include: new beginnings, stages of a woman's life, cycles (seasons, planting and harvesting, holidays, of emotions, weekday and Shabbat/weekend, high tide and low tide, etc.). This dance might be performed in the dark (perhaps outside, under the stars), using flashlights or candles as symbolic of light reflected off the moon. Accompaniment might be chanting or the recitation of Rosh Chodesh prayers.

Numbers
Advanced ■ ■ ■

Limits of Women's Vows

> But if her father restrains her on the day he finds out, none of her vows or self-imposed obligations shall stand; and God will forgive her. (Numbers 30:6)

Description

The 30th chapter of the Book of Numbers deals with vows. One verse (30:3) deals with a man's obligation to fulfill his vow (although no consequences are cited for his not fulfilling a vow). The rest of the chapter pertains to the vows made by women. The verse above describes how a woman's father (or husband) may annul her vow.

Motivating Movement

1. Have the group begin moving freely and confidently covering all the space in the room. Gradually decrease the amount of space in which each person may move. For example they may move in only one half of the room, then one fourth of the room, and then in only the small space around them. Coach the group to "want to move freely and confidently" even though the space has become limited.
2. Divide into pairs. One partner wants to cross the room, while the other partner's task is to restrain the partner from doing so. Some examples of safe methods of restraining are:

a. Facing each other, the restraining person puts his/her hands on the partner's hips and uses his/her weight to limit the partner's movement.
b. The restraining person holds one of the partner's ankles.
c. The restraining person stands behind the partner and holds onto the partner's waist.

This activity requires a sophisticated and very cooperative group, as the restraining person needs to be able to judge the appropriate weight to use in the activity. The person being restrained needs to be able to move somewhat, but not enough to accomplish the goal of crossing the room.

Dance Midrash

Have participants dance a woman's reaction to being restrained from fulfilling her vow by father or husband. First, have the group dance reactions of anger, resentment, and sad resignation at not fulfilling the vow. Next, have them experience relief and freedom because a burdensome vow has been eliminated. In a third improvisation, allow each participant to select his/her own reaction and expand on it.

Making Connections

Have the group discuss what it means to make a commitment, and share examples of commitments they make in their own lives. Some examples include:

Paying back someone on time

A pledge of behavior when joining a club or group

Marriage vows

Discuss the impact of not being able to fulfill a vow sincerely made because of someone else's control. What impact might that have on an individual's self-image?

Challenge

In the Bible, Hannah made a vow to God that if she conceived and bore a child, she would give the child to God as a priest (I Samuel 1:11). Hannah had a child and then fulfilled her vow by bringing her son to Shiloh to serve God.

In contrast to the Dance Midrash above when participants experienced the emotions of not being able to fulfill a vow, this challenge will give them an opportunity to experience fulfilling a commitment.

Together, read about Hannah in I Samuel. Discuss her strength of character. In *Eve's Journey*, Nehama Aschkenasy describes Hannah as single-minded, determined, and expressing passionate eloquence (Philadelphia: University of Pennsylvania Press, 1986).

Have participants create a movement portrait of Hannah.

Numbers
Intermediate ■ ■ ☐

Cities of Refuge

You shall provide yourselves with places to serve you as cities of refuge to which a manslayer who has killed a person unintentionally may flee. (Numbers 35:11)

Description

God instructed Moses to tell the Israelites to provide six cities as places of refuge. One who had accidentally killed another could find safety in one of these cities from those who might wish to avenge the victim's death.

Motivating Movement

1. Dancers imagine that they are punching bags. They move as if they are the recipients of continuous violent blows.
2. Dancers imagine that they are pillows in a gently sloping, grassy field. They roll calmly across the space as if through a place of refuge.

Making Connections

Discuss the following differing approaches to justice: innocent before proven guilty, and guilty before proven innocent. Discuss which type of justice the verse from Torah seems to support. (Note that Numbers 35:12 states: "The cities shall serve you as a refuge from the avenger, so that the manslayer may not die unless he has stood trial before the assembly.") Ask participants what an avenger might feel and what a manslayer might feel, and why it may be seen as a value to separate their respective polarities of emotion.

Dance Midrash

Divide the space into three areas:
- Scene of the (unintentional) crime
- Transition area through which the manslayer flees
- City of refuge

All dancers are (unintentional) manslayers. The object is for them to explore the quality of these three spaces by moving freely in and out of the spaces and changing their movement accordingly.

This improvisation is abstract—dancers do not need to follow any "logical" pattern as they go from one space to another. In fact, they should not all begin the improvisation in the same space.

Challenge

Divide into pairs: one is the manslayer, and one the avenger. The avenger is not a "real" avenger, but an avenger pictured in the mind of the manslayer, a figment of the manslayer's imagination. This improvisation focuses on the time when the manslayer is fleeing to the city of refuge. The manslayer improvises a dance of fleeing. The avenger dances as both the pursuer and the projected fear of the manslayer. In other words, the avenger should dance as if he/she is both separate from and part of the person of the manslayer. Switch roles and repeat.

Deuteronomy

Deuteronomy
Beginner ■ ☐ ☐

Moses' Final Address

These are the words that Moses addressed to all Israel.
(Deuteronomy 1:1)

Description

This is the beginning of the fifth and final book of Torah. It starts with a prologue in which Moses relates the recent history of the Israelites.

Motivating Movement

1. Have the group explore upper body movements, particularly movement developed by exaggerating gestures that a speaker/orator might make with hands, arms, shoulders, and head.
2. If a speaker's podium is available, have each person take a turn moving behind the podium, emphasizing upper body movements.
3. To reinforce moving only certain parts of the body, have the group experience using only legs and feet as gestures that accompany a speech.

Dance Midrash

Choreograph a phrase that captures the rhythm and importance conveyed by the verse above. Teach it to the group and have dancers accompany themselves by chanting the words in either English or Hebrew. Practice the phrase until everyone can do it confidently.

Each person then is to choose another phrase from the first three chapters of Deuteronomy and create a short dance to accompany that phrase. Some examples of phrases:

"You have stayed long enough at this mountain . . ."

"Go, take possession of the land that God swore to your ancestors . . ."

"God has multiplied you until you are today as numerous as the stars in the sky . . ."

"How can I bear unaided the trouble of you, and the burden, and the bickering . . ."

The group now chants and dances the phrase, "These are the words that Moses addressed to all Israel." Each person in turn presents an improvisation based on and accompanied by the words of his/her phrase. Between each person's improvisation, the group repeats, "These are the words Moses addressed to all Israel." Continue until all have danced their individual phrases.

Making Connections

Talk about the power an orator can have. Ask the group to share experiences of hearing a potent speaker and having been moved to action or inspired by the speaker's words. Point out that Deuteronomy contains Moses' oration to his people.

Challenge

When God first appeared to Moses in Exodus, Moses was reluctant to take on the role of leader. He replied to God, "Please, O Lord, I have never been a man of words, either in times past or now that You have spoken to Your servant; I am slow of speech and slow of tongue" (see Exodus 4:10).

In contrast, as leader of the Israelites during the forty years in the wilderness, Moses regularly addressed them. Aside from the Book of Deuteronomy, see also Moses' victory song in Exodus 15:1–19.

Have each person develop a dance study which shows Moses going from initial reluctance to dynamic addresses. In the dance movement, resolve whether Moses grows out of his speech impediment as he speaks regularly to the Israelites, learns how to deal with it, or continues to have a speaking problem. (See the "Dance Midrash" sections of "Let My People Go" and "Moses' Impediment," and the "Challenge" section of "The Burning Bush" for similar material.)

Deuteronomy
Intermediate ■ ■ □

Honor Father and Mother

> Honor your father and your mother, as God has commanded you, that you may long endure, and that you may fare well in the land that God is giving you. (Deuteronomy 5:16)

Description

The verse above contains the fifth of the Ten Commandments. Honoring parents is linked with living a good, long life in the new land. Underlying this commandment is the notion of Covenant—in response to God's gifts, we have responsibilities. In this case our responsibility is to honor God by honoring other human beings.

Motivating Movement

1. Have dancers create movements using their whole bodies and inspired by the following three gestures: serve food, plant a garden, open a book. Discourage pantomime.
    a. Dancers perform their gestures in a sloppy, resentful, and disrespectful manner.
    b. Dancers perform their gestures in a precise, positive, and respectful manner.
    c. Dancers repeat their gestures over and over again in a cycle, gradually moving from expressing disrespect to respect.

Making Connection

Have the group list *general* ways in which to honor parents. Then discuss the *specific* actions required in order to follow through on honoring. For example, what specific actions might be required in order to learn from and with parents, to help them maintain food and shelter for themselves and their family, to respect their values while trying to create their own identity and independence, to care for elderly parents, and to carry through on rituals for mourning parents who have died.

Dance Midrash

For honoring parents there is reward, a blessed life. Therefore, the command to honor parents invokes thankfulness for the opportunity for reward.

First, dancers create a movement phrase based on an "honoring parents" action of their choosing. (Refer to ideas generated by the group in the "Motivating Movement" and "Making Connections" sections above.) Then, after everyone has a phrase, the group improvises a dance expressing the tension between parental respect and disrespect. As they begin to resolve this tension, they then explore movement expressing thankfulness. Dancers should feel free to incorporate parts of others' phrases as they improvise.

Challenge

Each dancer creates a solo in which he/she is a forsaken parent. The emotions of being forsaken are the impetus for movement and might include: feelings of being rejected, deserted, dishonored, disappointed, angry.

As dancers experience these emotions, they should become more attuned to the reasons for the biblical emphasis on honoring one's parents.

Deuteronomy
Intermediate ■ ■ ☐

Hear, O Israel

Hear, O Israel! The Eternal is our God, the Eternal alone.
(Deuteronomy 6:4)

Description

These words (the *Shema*) communicated by Moses to the Israelite people are recited daily in the prayers of Jews everywhere. The *Shema* follows the Ten Commandments in the Torah and precedes the injunction to love God with all your heart, with all your soul, and with all your might.

Motivating Movement

1. Have dancers listen carefully to all kinds of sounds and silences, and improvise in response to what they hear. Examples of sounds include: music, words of a radio announcer, knocking, bells, hissing, clapping, a river, wind. Silences can be interspersed between sounds.

Making Connections

Discuss the difference between passive hearing and active listening. Ask for examples which illustrate the difference (see the poem "Listen" in the

"Challenge" section below). Which kind of listening was demanded of the Israelites?

Dance Midrash

1. Dancers take turns being Moses, while the rest are Israelites. Moses repeats the *Shema* several times over (in Hebrew or English) in a voice he/she feels carries the sense of the command. Dancers respond in movement in ways that reflect how they hear Moses' voice.

2. A Midrash suggests that the words of the *Shema* were spoken to Jacob (or Israel) by his sons as he was about to die—"Listen, Israel, we affirm and will carry on the belief in one God." Dancers take turns being Jacob (Israel) while the rest are Jacob's sons. The sons recite the *Shema* accompanied by improvised movement, as if they are at the side of the dying Jacob. Jacob responds in a way which reflects spiritual strength coupled with physical frailty.

Challenge

Have the group choreograph a dance about those who "hear—but do not really hear" and their transformation into those who do "hear." The following poem can be used as inspiration for the dance:

Listen!

Judaism begins with the commandment:
Hear, O Israel!
But what does it really mean to "hear?"
    The person who attends a concert
    With a mind on business,
    Hears—but does not really hear.
The person who walks amid the songs of birds
And thinks only of what will be served for dinner,
Hears—but does not really hear.
    The man who listens to the words of his friend,
    Or his wife, or his child,
    And does not catch the note of urgency:
    "Notice me, help me, care about me,"
    Hears—but does not really hear.
The person who listens to the news
And thinks only of how it will affect business,
Hears—but does not really hear.

The person who stifles the sound of conscience
And thinks "I have done enough already,"
Hears—but does not really hear.
The person who hears the Chazzan pray
And does not feel the call to join in prayer,
Hears—but does not really hear.
    The person who listens to the rabbi's sermon
    And thinks that someone else is being addressed,
    Hears—but does not really hear.
On this Shabbat, O Lord,
Sharpen our ability to hear.
May we hear the music of the world,
And the infant's cry, and the lover's sigh.
May we hear the call for help of the lonely soul,
And the sound of the breaking heart.
May we hear the words of our friends,

And also their unspoken pleas and dreams.
May we hear within ourselves the yearnings
That are struggling for expression.
May we hear You, O God.
For only if we hear You

Do we have the right to hope
That you will hear us.
Hear the prayers we offer to you this
day, O God,
And may we hear them too.

"Listen" by Jack Riemer and Harold Kushner. In *Likrat Shabbat* by Rabbis Sidney Greenberg and Jonathan D. Levine, published and copyrighted by The Prayerbook Press, 1363 Fairfield Ave., Bridgeport, CT 06605. Reprinted with permission.

Deuteronomy
Intermediate ■ ■ □

Teach with All Your Heart

> Take to heart these instructions with which I charge you this day.
> Impress them upon your children. (Deuteronomy 6:6–7)

Description

These verses spoken by Moses to the Israelites are a part of the daily Jewish liturgy known as the *Ve'ahavta*.

Motivating Movement

1. Divide into pairs. One person is to be the leader and the other the follower. They are to mirror each other moving slowly and carefully, making it hard to tell who is the leader and who the follower. Reverse roles and repeat as many times as desired.
2. Improvise movement which symbolizes casualness and contrast it with movement that symbolizes importance or extreme caring.

Making Connections

Ask each person to describe a teacher from whom he/she learned a lot. Ask what the teacher's method and manner of instruction were. Ask each person to share, leaving nameless, a teacher he/she disliked. Did he/she learn from that teacher as well? Discuss what the ideal teacher would be like.

Dance Midrash

Divide into pairs. One person is to teach an eight-count movement phrase to the other person. The pairs are to create an improvisation about the learning process as the phrase is learned. One person clearly portrays how important it is to teach the phrase and the other responds in relation to how he/she is being taught. Encourage the pairs to explore different ways of teaching such as:
   Teaching by example
   Dogmatic instruction during which the learner is told to do this or that
   Responding to the initiative of the learner
   Learning together
The learner can respond as he/she sees fit:
   Being eager to learn
   Being resistant and stubborn
   Being cooperative, but unenthusiastic
Reverse roles and repeat.

Challenge

1. Have a person who does sign language teach the group to sign the *Ve'ahavta* prayer (Deuteronomy 6:5–9). Once the actual signs are learned, each person is to expand the signed arm and hand gestures into larger body movements, creating a solo dance of the prayer.
2. Divide into quartets and have them create a dance inspired by the following passage from *Pirke Avot* 5:18 *(Ethics of the Fathers)*.

   There are four types among those who sit in the presence of sages: the sponge, the funnel, the strainer, and the sifter. The sponge soaks up everything. The funnel takes in at one end and lets out at the other. The strainer lets the wine pass and retains the dregs. The sifter holds back the coarse and collects the fine flour.

Deuteronomy
Beginner ■ ☐ ☐

The Hornets

God will send the hornet among them. (Deuteronomy 7:25)

Description

In the verse above, the Israelites were promised that God would send hornets to drive the Canaanites out of their hiding places. Out in the open the Canaanites would perish. The Israelites would then possess the land.

Motivating Movement

1. Have dancers find at least ten different hiding positions. Then, have them move furtively from one hiding position to another.
2. Have dancers imagine they are some kind of very irritating insect—hornet, mosquito, spider. Have them move through the space as if it were a crowded beach of sunbathers. Accompanying noises can be encouraged.

Dance Midrash

Divide the group into three parts—hornets, Canaanites, and Israelites. The Israelites gather on one edge of the space. The Canaanites hover together on the opposite side of the space. The hornets, beginning from an area next to the Israelites, "buzz" over to where the Canaanites are hiding. Without touching the Canaanites, the hornets drive out the Canaanites using movement and noises that are irritating, frightening, and threatening. When the Canaanites and hornets have dispersed offstage, the Israelites move freely and fully into the space. (Do the Israelites move cautiously, quickly, greedily, victoriously?) Repeat the improvisation at least three times in order that the dancers experience all three roles.

Find out how the dancers felt as they danced the three different roles. (Which role did they enjoy the most, the least, and why?)

Making Connections

The Israelites were told they were going to be in charge of a new land and that their enemies would disappear. At first, they were afraid and doubtful, but the help they were promised materialized and soon they entered the land and ruled it.

Ask dancers to think of a time when they felt they didn't have the ability to do something. How did they feel when they were encouraged and even pushed to go beyond their own expectations? How did they or would they feel if someone had gone ahead and made the way easier in order for them to accomplish that something? (Examples are giving a head start in a race, a parent helping a son or daughter get a job, drilling for a vocabulary test, throwing baseballs for practicing batting.) What are the limits for helping someone accomplish something?

Challenge

Again, divide group into three sections—Israelites, Canaanites, and doves. The Israelites and Canaanites begin on opposite sides of the space. There is a feeling of hostility between the two sides. The doves are in the center of the space. The role of the doves is to reconcile the two sides by encouraging them (through movement) to interact, to dance together in the whole space. Give each group the opportunity to dance the role of the doves. Ask dancers to compare their experience during this dance with the one they did in the "Dance Midrash" section. Did they prefer to be hornets or doves? Which scenario seems to reflect reality most accurately? What style of diplomacy would be most effective as a mediating force to use between warring peoples?

Deuteronomy
Intermediate ■ ■ □

Open Your Heart

> Circumcise the foreskin of your heart, and no longer be stiff-necked. (Deuteronomy 10:16)

Description

The Israelites were reminded by Moses that God required them to walk in God's ways, to love God, to serve God with heart and soul, and to follow God's commandments.

Motivating Movement

1. Have dancers move as stiffly as possible, as if they were made of wood.
2. Have dancers move in the most relaxed ways they can, as if they were made of pliable rubber.
3. Ask dancers to assume a position of "wooden" stiffness. Have them turn around slowly. With each revolution have them imagine they are peeling away a layer of stiffness, gradually moving from wood to pliable rubber.

Making Connections

Ask participants to think of a time when they felt stubborn or resistant about doing something they knew was the right thing to do (e.g., visiting someone in a nursing home, giving *tzedakah* [charity], inviting newcomers for dinner, resisting gossip, taking care of pets). Why did they resist doing the "right thing" even though they knew it was the right thing? How did they feel, or would they feel, if they did do what was right?

Dance Midrash

One dancer assumes the role of Moses communicating a message to the Israelites on behalf of God. The message is reflected in a phrase of movement that Moses repeats over and over as he tries to get the other dancers, the stiff-necked Israelites, to learn and to follow. At first, the Israelites are stubborn and don't pay attention to Moses' movement. As Moses appeals to them, some of them begin to respond by first learning part of Moses' danced message, and then by learning the whole phrase. Continue the improvisation until everyone is dancing the phrase together as a community. Repeat the improvisation, giving others an opportunity to dance the role of Moses.

Challenge

The group thinks of what types of forces destroy a community (crime, gossip, pollution, etc.). The group dances in unison a short phrase of movement while one to three dancers imagine they (together) form a particular destructive force. This "force" moves through the group, trying to distract members from following the community's phrase of movement. Continue the improvisation until all the dancers are moving randomly and separately.

Have participants compare their experience in this "Challenge" to that of the "Dance Midrash" above. What did they experience when they danced in unison as opposed to when they danced as separate individuals?

Deuteronomy
Intermediate ■ ■ □

Path to the Appointed Site

> But look only to the site that your God will choose amidst all your tribes as God's habitation, to establish God's name there. There you are to go. (Deuteronomy 12:5)

Description

In this part of Moses' message to the children of Israel, the emphasis was on unifying the religion by establishing a central sanctuary. This verse directly follows instructions to wipe out idolatry by destroying the images of other gods and the sites at which these gods were worshiped.

Motivating Movement

1. Draw a series of maps or have the group draw maps which show different routes to get to the central sanctuary.
   Each person takes a map and follows the route as directed, first walking and then adding movements of his/her choice. Have each person show his/her route to the rest of the group.

Dance Midrash

Designate an area in the dance space/classroom as the central sanctuary. Using the maps above, have everyone follow their route to the central sanctuary at the same time. Their intent is to come together to worship in this special place. They may add as much movement as they like as long as they follow the route on their maps. When they reach the sanctuary, they are to sit. The improvisation is over when everyone reaches the sanctuary and is sitting. Encourage the group to be aware of each other's paths and to feel free to move together when paths are the same. Intersecting paths can also motivate moving together.

Making Connections

Talk about places central to the worship of various religions. Share experiences, such as a trip to Israel, the Western Wall, the Vatican, Mecca, etc.

Challenge

1. Deuteronomy 16:1–17 includes instructions related to celebrating the three festival holidays. The emphasis is on gathering at the central sanctuary. Read the verses together and then divide the group into three sections. Each section is to take one of the holidays and create a dance which begins with the journey to the central place and continues with improvising on the celebration of the holiday in the sanctuary.
2. The Old City of Jerusalem is sacred for different religions. Have the group create a dance which visits any of the following places:

   The Western Wall where the Temple used to stand. Sacred to Jews.

   The stations of the cross where pilgrims retrace the stops that Jesus made on the way to his crucifixion. Sacred to Christians.

   The Dome of the Rock where Mohammed ascended into heaven and where the mysteries of revelation were disclosed to him. Sacred to Moslems.

Deuteronomy
Beginner ■ □ □

Sweep Out Evil

Thus you will sweep out evil from your midst. (Deuteronomy 13:6)

Description

The Israelites were warned not to listen to false prophets who taught or encouraged other forms of worship. Such prophets were to be put to death in order to keep evil away.

Motivating Movement

1. Have the group practice large, swinging movements.
2. Have the group improvise different ways to convey the word "sweep."

Dance Midrash

Divide the group. One half will be false prophets. The other half will be Israelites who "sweep evil" from their midst. The false prophets are to use a style of moving that is sustained and angular, while the Israelites are to use sweeping, swinging, and circular movements. At the beginning, both groups are to move in the entire space at the same time. Very gradually, the false prophet group is to be swept out of the center part of the space until they are only moving at the edges. Repeat, changing parts.

Making Connections

Discuss the kinds of influences which invite or encourage people to follow other religions. Some examples are: T.V. evangelism, the celebration of Christmas all around, and missionizers stopping people on the street. Ask the group to think of ways to maintain their own beliefs while respecting the rights of others to practice different religions. Ask how this kind of mutual respect contrasts with the situation in biblical times or in nonpluralistic societies.

Challenge

Divide the group into two. As in the "Dance Midrash" section above, one group will begin by representing the false prophets. They are to use contemporary influences as models for their movement (e.g., drug dealers selling drugs and promising great ecstasy from drugs). The other group, instead of sweeping the "false prophets" out of their space, "sweeps" them out of influencing them or out of selling what they have to offer. Once both groups have clearly established who they are, call out "Change roles." Immediately, without stopping, the dancers are to change to the opposite role. Repeat, calling "Change roles" with varying periods of time in between.

Deuteronomy
Intermediate ■ ■ ☐

Do Not Deviate

You must not deviate from the verdict that they announce to you either to the right or to the left. (Deuteronomy 17:11)

Description

The Israelites were told to bring baffling judicial cases to the Levitical priests or the magistrate in charge. In other words, such cases were to be brought to those who served as a "higher court." Those who brought a case were to follow scrupulously the decisions announced to them.

Motivating Movement

1. Movements to try on both a curvy/zigzag line and along a straight line are:
   a. 4 large steps forward, 4 small backward, repeating
   b. Skipping
   c. Walking "on all fours" (hands and feet)
   d. Moving forward while rotating

Making Connections

Have the group come up with a controversy involving two people (perhaps having to do with real estate, money, or love). What good advice could a third party give in order to resolve the controversy? What would be the benefits of following the third party's advice? What would happen if after receiving the advice, one or both of the people deviated from the instructions given to them? Taking this issue a step further, discuss the value of having higher courts make firm decisions on baffling matters.

Dance Midrash

Half the dancers are "baffled" by a controversy and half are Levitical priests (higher court officials). The halves begin on opposite sides of the room. The baffled dancers move across the space toward the priests in ways which reflect their confusion. When they approach the priests, the priests begin interacting with them. The goal of the priests is to lead the baffled dancers into clear, precise movement, i.e., movement that does not deviate "either to the left or to the right." The priests may use physical contact and/or example to instruct the baffled dancers. Repeat improvisation, switching roles.

Challenge

1. Dancers perform solo improvisations in which they explore in depth aspects of being baffled, contrasted with "following a straight line." They should pick two words which characterize these opposite states. These pairs of words will stimulate and be explored in the improvisation. Examples of word pairs are:

   Confused and clear

   Frustrated and encouraged

   Cloudy and enlightened

   Imprecise and precise

   Stumped and discovering

   Muddy and lucid

   Vague and determined

   Observers should pay attention to the nuances being expressed in each dancer's improvisation.
2. Dancers explore the tension between:
   a. Feeling dissatisfied with a verdict given for a baffling problem and
   b. Struggling to stay on the "straight path."
   Note that dissatisfaction may involve resistance, resentment, and/or discomfort.

Deuteronomy
Intermediate ■ ■ □

Protecting Trees During War

> When in your war against a city you have to besiege it a long time in order to capture it, you must not destroy its trees, wielding the ax against them. (Deuteronomy 20:19)

Description

The Israelites were given instructions concerning appropriate conduct during war. In the verse above, they were told that even when making war, they must protect the trees . . .

Motivating Movement

1. Bring in pictures of different kinds of trees, such as tall redwoods, olive trees, Joshua trees, aspens, oak trees, and willows. Ask each person to choose one of the trees and to improvise movement "in place" which captures the unique quality of the tree. Repeat with each person selecting a different tree to portray.
2. Have the group practice large percussive movement which conveys waging war, besieging a city, and wielding an ax. Contrast this with movement which protects and nurtures the natural environment.

Dance Midrash

Divide participants into groups of about six dancers. Each group is to imagine they are Israelites trying to capture an enemy's city while protecting the trees. On large pieces of drawing paper, have the groups map out the space, indicating where the trees they plan to protect are located, as well as where the buildings they plan to capture and destroy are located. When they have a clear visual image of the space, have them dance their plan. Coach them to contrast their movements in the areas to be protected with their movements in the areas where structures are to be destroyed.

Making Connections

In Jewish tradition, trees symbolize life, continuity of generations, and Torah. Ask what other religious or symbolic significance trees might have. How can understanding such symbolism deepen a respect for trees?

Challenge

Meditations have often been inspired by the letters in God's name (*Yod, Hay, Vav, Hay*). Have the group develop the following 5-phrase dance meditation, using imagery on trees and the letters in God's name.

Phrase 1—represents the *Yod* as a tiny seed leading into the *Hay*

Phrase 2—the *Hay*, flowing and curving expanse of roots

Phrase 3—the *Vav*, a tall trunk

Phrase 4—the *Hay*, a flowing curving expanse of branches

Phrase 5—a transition back to the *Yod* (i.e., a seed coming from the fruit or branch)

Have each person share his/her solo and encourage each person to have his/her own unique interpretation of the images.

Note: This idea was inspired by Arthur Waskow in his book *Seasons of Our Joy* (New York: Bantam Books, 1982), 112.

Deuteronomy
Beginner ■ □ □

Regard for Animals

If along the road you chance upon a bird's nest, in any tree or on the ground, with fledglings or eggs and the mother sitting over the fledglings or on the eggs, do not take the mother together with her young. Let the mother go, and take only the young, in order that you may fare well and have a long life. (Deuteronomy 22:6–7)

Description

Regard for animals in the Torah is exemplified by the commandment in the verse above. To take a mother bird's eggs or fledglings from right before her eyes would be cruel. Kindness is what God requires and what God rewards.

Motivating Movement

1. Ask dancers to think of a treasured stuffed animal or doll, blanket, book, letter, pet, or other special possession.
   a. Have them imagine they are holding the object and dancing with it protectively, lovingly, with care.
   b. Have them adjust their movement with the imagined object as if someone were trying to take the treasured object away from them.
2. Have dancers practice bird-like movements.

Making Connections

Lead a discussion on cruelty to animals. Have the participants share examples of such actions. How do they feel when they see people being mean to animals? Talk about what kind of feelings animals might have and the responsibilities we have to respect those.

Dance Midrash

Designate for each dancer a small space on the floor which will symbolize his or her "nest" containing three baby birds. They begin by dancing protectively (with bird-like movements) around their nests. After they have established a feeling of protection around their nests, the leader will go around to each "bird" and symbolically take away the baby birds. The dancer will dance his/her reactions, as the leader moves on to another bird.

Challenge

Have dancers, either individually or in pairs, come up with their own law for the prevention of cruelty to animals. Have them make up a phrase of movement expressing that law and present it to the rest of the group.

As an extension of the challenge, the dancers can create a booklet of illustrations for the laws presented in dance.

Deuteronomy
Beginner ■ ☐ ☐

Land of Milk and Honey

> God has brought us to this place, given us this land, a land flowing with milk and honey. (Deuteronomy 26:9)

Description

God brought the Israelites from Egypt, the land of their slavery, to a land of abundance.

Motivating Movement

1. Have dancers practice the following types of movements across the space: rolling, somersaults, spinning, and twirling.
2. To experience the different elements of the landscape, dancers first become one element and then change into another. Ask them to begin to move as if they are rocks, then to become trees, hills, and finally valleys. The leader calls out the elements as the dancers move.

Dance Midrash

Divide the group into pairs. Each pair identifies itself as a tree, rock, hill, or valley, and creates together a position suggesting the object. The partners should be physically connected, touching in some way. The pairs are spread out in the space.

As the improvisation begins, one partner imagines being a sweet and delicious substance (symbolic of the milk and honey). He/she detaches from the other partner with flowing, rolling movements. The "sweet and delicious" dancers flow through and around their "landscape" partners who have remained still. After finishing a tour through the "land" (i.e., the other dancers in the entire space), the flowing, sweet and delicious dancers (in their own time) return to and reconnect with partners. It is not necessary to return to the same partner after each "tour" through the land. The still partner and the sweet and delicious partner switch roles. Repeat as many times as desired.

Making Connections

Have dancers imagine a fantasy candyland—chocolate rivers, cotton candy trees, ice cream ski slopes, licorice highways, gingerbread houses with sponge cake garages, etc. Imagine coming to this land after years and years of a bland diet—manna and water. How would they react?

To the Israelites, Israel was like a dreamland after having wandered forty years in the wilderness. In Israel they were blessed with abundance. Many modern-day immigrants to Israel have similar feelings, especially those who have suffered greatly (in concentration camps, as persecuted minorities in Arab countries, as victims of famine and discrimination in Ethiopia).

Challenge

Some of the present-day products "flowing" out of Israel are oranges, almonds, olives, tomatoes, flowers, books, building stones, designer clothing, and Jewish ritual objects. Israel's contemporary landscape consists of buildings, orchards, farms, highways, and piers. Using the model in the Dance Midrash above, recreate the improvisation based on Israel's present-day landscape and products. Coach dancers to move in ways that reflect the modern Israel as contrasted to the movement qualities they used to portray the biblical landscape.

Deuteronomy
Intermediate ■ ■ □

A Holy People

> You will be established as God's holy people, as was sworn to you, if you keep the commandments of your God and walk in God's ways. And all the peoples of the earth shall see that God's name is proclaimed over you, and they shall stand in fear of you.
> (Deuteronomy 28:9–10)

Description

Essentially, the above verses tell Israel that they will be God's holy people and that other peoples will notice and watch them.

Motivating Movement

1. Practice mirroring movement:
   a. Divide into pairs. Have one partner mirror the movements of the other. Begin slowly with simple arm movements and gradually involve more of the bodies. Change roles.
   b. Divide the group. Each half decides on a sequence of five or so movements (e.g., circle head, roll shoulders, twist waist, stamp right foot twice, and jump-turn to the right). As one half performs their sequence several times over in unison, the second half tries to follow along as closely as possible. Repeat, with the other half leading their sequence.
2. Have the group explore evil and righteousness in movement:
   a. Evil—low to the ground, contracted, and hovering movement
   b. Righteousness—tall, centered, and exalted movement

Dance Midrash

Divide the group. Each half decides on a sequence of counts in which the movement will go back and forth from expressing evil to expressing righteousness (e.g., 8 counts evil, 4 counts righteousness, 4 counts evil, 8 counts righteousness). The first half, Israel improvises according to its sequence of counts (repeated several times over). The second half, other peoples who express the ways Israel influences them, try to pick up Israel's pattern of counts and follow the types of movements being expressed. Repeat, with the other half being Israel and leading their sequence.

Making Connections

Ask dancers what they experienced in the Dance Midrash. Was it easy or difficult for the "other peoples" to be influenced by what "Israel" was doing? What does it mean to be a "holy people" or nation? When would a holy people cease being holy? Are there any holy peoples or nations in the world today? What makes them holy, and how do they influence other nations? The term *Or la'goyim*, "a light unto the nations," is a term applied to Israel's role during biblical times. In what ways is the modern state of Israel an *Or la'goyim*, and what must it do in order to sustain that role?

Challenge

Build on the discussion in the "Making Connections" section above by having participants improvise a dance in which they struggle to become a "holy people." Based on the last question in that section, emphasize the difficulties involved in becoming an *Or la'goyim*. Each participant takes a specific role to portray in the improvisation (e.g., "secular" Israeli, ultra-Orthodox Jew, *kibbutznik*, West Bank settler, left wing radical, soldier, and politician). Before dancing, have each person think about and share movement possibilities for his/her role.

Deuteronomy
Advanced ■ ■ ■

Return to God

Return to God with all your heart and soul. (Deuteronomy 30:10)

Description

The verse above comes from Moses' final address to the children of Israel wherein he reminded them of their escape from Egypt, their wandering in the desert, and their covenant with God. Moses cautioned that they would be cursed if their hearts turned from God to worship the gods of other nations. In contrast, he promised that they would be blessed with abundance when they returned to God.

Motivating Movement

1. Have the group experiment with different ways of turning. Ask them to pay attention to how they prepare for the turn and how they gain momentum while turning. Divide the group into sections and watch each other's turns. Have the observers comment on what they saw.
2. If someone in the group is trained in classical ballet, ask him/her to demonstrate different preparations for turns and to teach them to the group.
3. Conclude by asking the group to do turns motivated by:

a. A plié or downward motion
b. Stepping onto the ball of their foot
c. Swinging an arm
d. Contracting

Dance Midrash

This improvisation is based on Martin Buber's view that God is present to us through our interactions with each other. Ask participants to begin isolated from each other (as in doing something displeasing to God). Gradually, the participants come together, aware of their sincere desire to return to God by being part of a community, and behaving in a manner which is pleasing to God. Have them make use of the different kinds of turns which they practiced earlier. The improvisation ends when everyone is part of a group moving together.

Making Connections

Ask participants to think about a time when they felt isolated. Perhaps they were disappointed with themselves because they had done something wrong. How did they regain confidence and feel good about themselves again?

Ask participants to reflect on a time when they felt dissatisfied with their religious identity. Has it ever been a burden? How did they resolve this feeling? How did their behavior change?

Challenge

Ask participants to think of the prayer which most inspires them. They are to pretend they haven't heard the prayer or said it for several years because they have lost faith or turned away from their religion. Now they are returning to a service, perhaps out of curiosity or because of a need to reaffirm their faith. They are to improvise on their reactions as they hear this special prayer again. Have each person share his/her dance with the group. The group says or sings the prayer to accompany the improvisation. (The prayer can be repeated as many times as necessary until the dancer completes the improvisation.)

Deuteronomy
Intermediate ■ ■ □

God's Hidden Countenance

> *I will abandon them and hide my countenance from them.*
> (Deuteronomy 31:17)

Description

God said that after Moses died, the Israelites would go astray and break the covenant that God had made with them. Then God's anger would flare up against them.

Motivating Movement

1. Have dancers explore in movement the act of abandoning. Have them try to come up with as many different ways of abandoning as they can and to reflect those nuances in their movement (e.g., violent, regretful, angry, indifferent, tragic).
2. Have dancers explore being abandoned, again with many different nuances (e.g., with hurt, relief, surprise, anger, indifference, hysteria).

Dance Midrash

Dancers choose a style of movement that will represent the right or "covenantal" way to be, for example, dancing upright. They then identify which movement will represent its opposite, for example, movement on the floor. As dancers gradually move from "right" to "wrong" movement, they express their feelings as God's countenance "shines upon them" and then turns and hides from them. In other words, they express in dance feelings of wholeness that turn into feelings of abandonment.

Making Connections

Ask dancers to imagine playing hide and seek with their friends. It is their turn to hide and wait for the others to find them. They wait and wait, but nothing seems to be happening. When they finally emerge from their places, they realize that no one has even looked for them. How do they feel? Perhaps this is what is meant by the verse above—that God is waiting and ready for people to seek God out, but they do not do so. Thus people, by their actions (or inaction), keep God in hiding.

Challenge

In Genesis we read that we are created in the image of God. If this is so, it is conceivable to interpret the verse above to mean that in some way we are hidden from ourselves. Parts of ourselves are unaware and unconscious. In what ways do we alienate ourselves from ourselves (through self-deception, shallowness, stubbornness, narrow-mindedness, envy, etc.)? In the improvisation have dancers seek out and explore that which in themselves has been abandoned and hidden.

Deuteronomy
Advanced ■ ■ ■

Like an Eagle

Like an eagle who rouses its nestlings, gliding down to its young, so did God spread wings and take [Israel] along, bearing [Israel] on God's pinions. (Deuteronomy 32:11)

Description

In Moses' last poetic song to Israel, he compared God to an eagle and Israel to the eagle's nestlings. As an eagle cares for its young, so, too, did God nurture Israel in its youth. This nurturing provided shelter and security, as well as guidance.

Motivating Movement

1. Have dancers practice soaring and gliding movements. At first, have them try to convey as much strength as they can in their soaring. Then have them try to convey gentleness. Finally, have them soar in ways that express both strength and gentleness.
2. Ask dancers to be eagles. Their arms are eagles' wings. Have them experiment with bird-like movements. Ask the dancers to move as if they are eagles caring for their young, feeding and protecting them.

Making Connections

In verse 10 we read that God found Israel in a desert region, in an empty, howling waste. God took Israel from there as if on the spread wings of an eagle. Discuss times when individuals have become stranded and lost in some desolate area for days, weeks, and even months (for example, after a plane crash that took place in the Andes). Ask dancers how they would feel if they were an individual who, after being stranded for a long time, was spotted by an airplane and rescued.

Dance Midrash

Have half the group be Israel (the nestlings) and the other half be forces that are nurturing and strong (the eagles). The Israelites begin by dancing a dance of desolation, as if the space were an empty, howling waste. As they are dancing, the nurturing and strong forces move toward them. These forces want to move the Israelites in such a way as to guide them on a special journey. What happens on this journey (guidance toward freedom, spiritual discipline, specific commandments, self-reliance, victory in battles, etc.) is something for the forces to consider as they lead the Israelites. How responsive are the Israelites? Repeat the improvisation, switching roles.

Challenge

There is a morning prayer which contains much vivid imagery, including that of eagles' wings. Create a dance based on the following prayer:

> Though our mouths should overflow with song as the sea, our tongues with melody as the roaring waves, our lips with praise as the heavens' wide expanse; and though our eyes were to shine as the sun and the moon, our arms extend like eagles' wings, our feet speed swiftly as deer—still we could not fully thank You, Lord our God and God of all ages, or bless Your name enough, for even one of Your infinite kindnesses to our ancestors and to us.

Reprinted with permission from *Gates of Prayer: The New Union Prayerbook*. © 1975 Central Conference of American Rabbis, New York, and Union Liberal and Progressive Synagogues, London, 298.

Deuteronomy
Beginner ■ □ □

Israel: Fat and Kicked

So Jeshurun grew fat and kicked. . . . (Deuteronomy 32:15)

Description

In Moses' last words to Israel, he prophesied that in spite of God's guidance and nurturing, Israel (Jeshurun) would become oversatisfied, spoiled, and stubborn as a kicking mule.

Motivating Movement

1. Begin by having the dancers walk normally. Then have them do the walk in an exaggerated, ugly, and offensive way. Repeat with running, jumping, and skipping.
2. Have dancers practice all kinds of ways to kick. Then, have them take that same energy into other parts of their bodies, making kick-like movements with their arms, heads, hips, shoulders, elbows.

Making Connections

Discuss a time when group members were told not to do something that they wanted to do and were also told that this instruction was for their own good.

Did they rebel? What did they do when they realized in retrospect that the instruction really was for the best?

Dance Midrash

There are three elements in this improvisation:

The dancers imagine they are Israelites enjoying life in the Promised Land, but also following a specific code of behavior. Their movement will be clean, precise, pleasing.

The movement becomes more exaggerated, sloppy, offensive.

The Israelites rebel and express their haughtiness and stubbornness by doing kick-like movements.

Challenge

Repeat the improvisation from the "Dance Midrash." This time, have half the dancers take the role of the prophet Isaiah who expressed his message to the Israelites by scolding, warning, threatening, and expressing anguish. For example, he exclaimed:

Ah, sinful nation! People laden with iniquity! Brood of evildoers! Depraved children! They have forsaken the Lord, spurned the Holy One of Israel, turned their backs [on God]. (Isaiah 1:4)

In another verse Isaiah called Israel into action:

Learn to do good. Devote yourselves to justice; aid the wronged. Uphold the rights of the orphan; defend the cause of the widow. (Isaiah 1:17)

The other half of the dancers represent the community. Change roles.

Deuteronomy
Advanced ■ ■ ■

God's Everlasting Arms

God is a refuge, a support are the arms everlasting. (Deuteronomy 33:27)

Description

As part of Moses' farewell, he blessed the Israelites, addressing each tribe. The words in the verse above were directed to the tribe of Asher.

Motivating Movement

1. Have dancers try to discover all the different ways arms can move (e.g., reaching, stretching, pulling, pushing, swinging, enveloping, twisting, circling, elbowing, etc.). Coach dancers to use the arms as initiating a second movement, such as a turn, roll, jump, or leap.
2. Have dancers imagine they are walking across a tightrope (one at a time). First they walk as if there is nothing underneath them except the ground below and second, as if they cannot fall, as if there are arms that would catch them were they to wobble. Have them be conscious of how they use their arms as they traverse the imaginary tightrope.
3. Give dancers the experience of being carried by arms:

a. Two dancers cross their arms and grab hands with each other. (Each should have the same arm on top so that the arms are "locked" together.) They then carry a third dancer. Switch roles.
b. Two dancers face each other. Each stretches out the left arm, bends the right arm, and with the right hand holds onto the middle of his/her own left arm. Then, with the left hand, each holds onto the bent lower part of the partner's right arm (near the elbow). They then carry a third dancer. Switch roles.
c. The following should be done only with a cautious and well-supervised group:
Dancers line up in two rows facing each other. Each dancer stretches out his/her arms and holds hands with the person opposite. One dancer begins at one end of the rows and lies down on the arms. The arms move up and down until the person is "bounced" to the opposite end. Switch roles.
4. Have dancers improvise as if on the wings of an airplane. Have them begin while the plane is standing still and dance the taxiing, takeoff, flight, and landing.

Dance Midrash

In groups of 4–5, choreograph three different falls, one dancer falling, the rest catching. Include more than one step, such as fall and roll, fall and contract, fall and collapse.

One person will do the falling and will improvise transitional movement between the previously choreographed falls. The transitional movement should be motivated by the idea of traveling through a dangerous world. The others will follow with their "supportive arms" ready to catch when the one dancer falls. That dancer then recovers and continues traveling. Repeat until everyone has had the opportunity to be the one who falls.

Making Connections

Ask the group when the physical support of arms is most comforting and reassuring (e.g., when a child falls and gets hurt, someone is grieving over a painful loss, etc.). Ask what emotions are evoked by the image of God as everlasting supportive arms.

Challenge

1. Elevate ordinary arm movements to represent a nurturing community. Arms should interact and be supportive in ways that reflect the ideal community, i.e., the arms should be physically, emotionally, and spiritually supportive. As dancers improvise and create their network of arms, coach them to change back and forth from supporter to one in need of support.
2. The image of "arms" has another connotation, that of weapons. Have the group improvise a dance in which half portrays arms as supports and half portrays arms as weapons. How do the different kinds of arms interact (or do they)?

Deuteronomy
Intermediate ■ ■ ☐

Moses Sees the Promised Land

> And the Lord said to him, "This is the land of which I swore to Abraham, Isaac, and Jacob. I will give it to your offspring. I have let you see it with your own eyes, but you shall not cross there."
> (Deuteronomy 34:4)

Description

Moses was not to enter the Land of Israel. However, standing on a summit of a mountain, he saw the Promised Land from afar before he died.

Motivating Movement

1. Ask dancers to imagine they are on a mountaintop. They have very limited space in which to move and are looking out over the most beautiful landscape they have ever seen. Coach them to experiment with movement which takes in the view and is very expansive while they remain in the limited space.
2. Have dancers improvise on the feeling of disappointment.

Making Connections

Lead a discussion about achieving goals. Talk about the feeling of satisfaction in reaching a goal. Ask, "How do you feel when you realize you will not reach a goal you have established?"

Dance Midrash

Portray Moses on the summit as he sees the Land of Israel. Convey the various emotions which he feels at that moment. In particular, contrast the joy of "seeing with your own eyes" to the disappointment of "you shall not cross there." Which emotion dominates and ends the improvisation?

Challenge

1. There are many Midrashim centered on the moment when Moses saw the Land of Israel and made a final plea to God to allow him to enter the land. The dancers are Moses. They feel sure God will relent and grant their wish. Each creates a dance which begs God to show mercy as God has so often in the past. Remind them that because Moses' desire is so great, he would be as persuasive as possible—pleading, asking forgiveness for sins, reviewing his life, pointing out his strengths.

   After everyone is done improvising and sharing his/her improvisations, list all the different arguments that the group discovered through dance. Compare these with some of the traditional Midrashim. For examples of these, see *The Torah: A Modern Commentary*, edited by W. Gunther Plaut (New York: Union of American Hebrew Congregations, 1981), 1585–6.

2. In Numbers 14:20–45 we learn that Moses was not the only one prevented from entering the Promised Land. A whole rebellious generation died in the wilderness without arriving there.

   Have the group choreograph a short dance (about 3 minutes) on the theme of journeying. Emotions that might motivate the choreographed movement might include hope, anxiety, excitement, weariness, and/or doubt.

   Have the group perform the dance several times. With each repetition designate small areas of the space which dancers imagine to be on fire. They have to continue dancing as well as they can while avoiding the "burning" spaces. As more spaces "burn," the choreography will disintegrate.

   This Challenge is appropriate for *Tisha B'Av*, as the symbolic burning of spaces represents the literal and figurative burning of hopes, dreams, and creativity that occurred on that day.

Appendix I

HOLIDAYS AND LIFE EVENTS:
SUGGESTED DANCE MIDRASHIM

The following Dance Midrashim are appropriate and can be adapted for teaching about or celebrating various holidays and life events. Some adaptations will be obvious; others call for a bit of creativity.

HOLIDAYS
Shabbat
    Light from Darkness (Genesis 1:4)   3
    First Shabbat (Genesis 2:2)   7
    Keep the Sabbath (Exodus 20:8)   98

Rosh Chodesh
    New Moons (Numbers 28:11)   195

Rosh Hashanah/Yom Kippur
    Scapegoat (Leviticus 16:21)   146
    Sound the Shofar (Leviticus 25:9)   159
    Return to God (Deuteronomy 30:10)   232
    God's Hidden Countenance (Deuteronomy 31:17)   234

Appendix I

Sukkot
    Etrog, Palm, Myrtle, and Willow (Leviticus 23:40) — 156

Simchat Torah
    Shouldering the Sacred (Numbers 7:9) — 175

Chanukah
    Giving (Exodus 25:1–2) — 107

Tu B'Shevat
    Protecting Trees during War (Deuteronomy 20:19) — 224

Purim
    Jacob: One who Disguises (Genesis 27:19) — 36

Pesach
    Let My People Go (Exodus 5:1) — 80
    Leaving Egypt (Exodus 12:11) — 89
    Crossing the Sea (Exodus 14:22) — 94

Yom HaShoah
    A New Pharaoh Deals Harshly (Exodus 1:10) — 73

Yom HaAtzma'ut
    Land of Milk and Honey (Deuteronomy 26:9) — 228

Tisha B'Av
    Moses Sees the Promised Land (Deuteronomy 34:4) — 243

LIFE EVENTS

Birth
    Fill the Earth (Genesis 1:28) — 5

Bar/Bat Mitzvah
    Teach With All Your Heart (Deuteronomy 6:6–7) — 212

Conversion
    Abram, Go Forth (Genesis 12:1) — 17

Appendix I

Marriage
    Sister . . . Let Me Live (Genesis 12:13)   19

Death
    Sarah's Lifetime (Genesis 23:1)   29
    Isaac Dies (Genesis 35:28–29)   50
    Joseph Mourns His Father (Genesis 50:10)   68

Appendix II
RESOURCES FOR LEADING SESSIONS

ITEMS TO COLLECT

Accessories
    "Dress-up Box" (Costumes)
    Pieces of Fabric (Different Sizes and Textures)
    Ribbons
    Ritual Objects (Prayer Shawl, Candle Sticks)
    Scarves

Files of Pictures
    Animals
    Architecture
    Colors
    Museum Prints/Postcards
    Photographs
    Shapes
    Trees

Flash Cards
   Adjectives (e.g., aggressive, proud, shy, tense)
   Adverbs (e.g., desperately, quickly, slowly)
   Emotions (e.g., anger, joy, sadness)
   Opposites (e.g., high/low, relaxed/tense, strong/weak)
   Verbs (e.g., leap, run, skip)

Miscellaneous
   Box of Instruments (see next section for ideas)
   Butcher Paper
   Newspaper
   Parachute

ITEMS TO ACCOMPANY DANCING

Box of Instruments
   Bells, castanets, cymbals, drums, horns, kazoos, pots and pans, recorder, hakers, shofar, tambourines, triangles, etc.

Sound Effects (Actual or Recorded)
   Baby crying, conversations, doorbells, echoes, insects, rivers, thunder, urban sounds, water running, wind rustling, etc.

Recorded Music
   Classical, electronic, folk, jazz, "new age," religious, rock, etc.

Voiced Music
   Chanting, crying, hissing, poetry, prayers, prose, screams, song, whispering, etc.

Appendix III

HOW TO ASK QUESTIONS

Types of questions are followed by examples. Examples are general and do not follow a particular order. To make this section most useful, refer to it with a specific Dance Midrash in mind and try to come up with appropriate questions for teaching sections of that exercise.

FROM GENERAL TO SPECIFIC
World
"How might world religions help bring about international peace?"

Between Two Nations
"How might Arabs and Jews (or Canaanites and Israelites) live together in peace?"

Communal
"When the Israelites were in the wilderness, how did they maintain peace with the community?"

Personal
"What experiences make you feel most at peace within yourself?"

FROM ANCIENT TO MODERN
Ancient
"How did the ancient Israelites handle the situation?"

Modern
"How might modern Israelis handle the same situation?"

"WHAT IF" QUESTIONS
Situational and Personal
"What if you were in such and such a situation?" or "What if you were in so and so's shoes?"

Ascribing Unnatural Qualities to Various Things
"What if the rock that Moses struck could speak—what would it say?"

Considering the Unlikely and the Impossible
"What if Moses had never come back from the top of Mount Sinai?"

WHAT ARE THE LIMITS
Emotional
"How ecstatic can you make Sarah's joy?"

Physical
"How far can you lean before you are off balance?"

Qualitative
"How fast can you go? How slow?"

SUGGESTING OPTIONS
Emotional
"How did Moses feel? Was he happy, relieved, secretly annoyed?"

Physical
"Did Moses run away after speaking with Pharaoh? Walk confidently? Stumble?"

Qualitative
"Would Moses have moved in a strong or gentle fashion?"

Appendix III

EXHAUSTING POSSIBILITIES/BRAINSTORMING
Examples

"Name *every* biblical character who struggled with a sibling relationship."

"What are *all* the possible ways the characters in Genesis could have dealt more effectively with a sibling?"

Appendix IV

DANCE MIDRASHIM BY TORAH PORTION

GENESIS
Beresheet
    Light from Darkness   3
    Fill the Earth   5
    First Shabbat   7
    Naming the Creatures   9
    Discovery   11

Noah
    Bursting of the Floodgates   13
    Gibberish   15

Lech Lecha
    Abram, Go Forth   17
    Sister . . . Let Me Live!   19

Vayera
    Sarah Laughed   21

Lot's Wife	23
Hagar's Eyes Are Opened	25
The Binding of Isaac	27

Chayay Sarah
Sarah's Lifetime	29
Rebekah's Veil	32

Toledot
Jacob Emerges	34
Jacob: One Who Disguises	36

Vayeytze
Jacob's Dream	39
Jacob's Journey Continues	41
Sisters: Leah and Rachel	43

Vayishlach
Jacob Wrestles	45
Dinah	47
Isaac Dies	50

Vayeshev
Joseph Dreams	52
Joseph Is Cast into the Pit	54
Judah's Pledge to Tamar	56

Miketz
Joseph in Charge	58
Joseph Names His Sons	60

Vayigash
Egyptians Become Serfs	63

Vayechi
Blessing Ephraim and Manasseh	65
Joseph Mourns His Father	68

EXODUS
Shmot
A New Pharaoh Deals Harshly	73

The Burning Bush	76
Moses Stands on Holy Ground	78
Let My People Go	80

Vaera
Moses' Impediment	82
Frogs Everywhere	85
Darkness Descends on Egypt	87

Bo
Leaving Egypt	89
Sign and Symbol of Freedom	92

Beshalach
Crossing the Sea	94
Hands of Victory	96

Yitro
Keep the Sabbath	98
Amazement at Sinai	100

Mishpatim
Helping Your Enemy	102
Against Cruelty	105

Terumah
Giving	107
Winged Cherubim	109
Colored Gate	111

Tetzaveh
Anointment	113

Ki Tisa
The Lure of Gold	115
Moses Sees the Golden Calf	117
God Shields Moses	119

Vayakhel
Excellence for the Tabernacle	121

Pekuday
    Levels of Sacred Space   123
    The Cloud and God's Presence   125

LEVITICUS
Vayikrah
    An Offering by Fire   129
    Drawing Near   131

Tsav
    Holy on Contact   133
    Blood Ritual   136

Shemini
    They Saw and Shouted   138

Tazriya
    Unclean! Unclean!   140
    Contaminated Fabric   142

Metzora
    A Plague in the House   144

Acharay Mot
    Scapegoat   146
    Defiling the Land   148

Kedoshim
    Leave Some for the Poor   150
    Stumbling Blocks   152
    Love the Stranger   154

Emor
    Etrog, Palm, Myrtle, and Willow   156
    Sound the Shofar   159

Behar
    The Jubilee Year   161

Bechukotai
    Reward and Punishment   163
    Clearing Out the Old   166

NUMBERS

Bemidbar
    In the Wilderness — 171

Naso
    Blessing of Peace — 173
    Shouldering the Sacred — 175

Beha'alotecha
    The Wave — 177
    Miriam Stricken — 179

Shelach Leecha
    Fringed Reminder — 181

Korach
    Moses Hears and Falls — 183

Chukat
    Striking the Rock — 185
    Copper Serpent — 187

Balak
    Balaam Blesses — 189
    Flaunting Leads to Death — 191

Pinchas
    Daughters of Zelophehad — 193
    New Moons — 195

Matot
    Limits of Women's Vows — 197

Mas'ay
    Cities of Refuge — 200

DEUTERONOMY

Devarim
    Moses' Final Address — 205

Va'etchanan
    Honor Father and Mother — 207

Appendix IV

Hear, O Israel	209
Teach With All Your Heart	212

Ekev
The Hornets	214
Open Your Heart	216

Re'eh
Path to the Appointed Site	218
Sweep Out Evil	220

Shofetim
Do Not Deviate	222
Protecting Trees During War	224

Ki Tetze
Regard for Animals	226

Ki Tavo
Land of Milk and Honey	228
A Holy People	230

Nitzavim
Return to God	232

Vayelech
God's Hidden Countenance	234

Ha'azinu
Like an Eagle	236
Israel: Fat and Kicked	238

V'zot HaBerachah
God's Everlasting Arms	240
Moses Sees the Promised Land	243

Sources Related To Midrash

Torah Translations/Bibles

The New Jerusalem Bible. Garden City, NY: Doubleday and Company, Inc., 1985.

The New Oxford Annotated Bible with the Apocrypha, Revised Standard Version. Herbert G. May and Bruce M. Metzger, eds. New York: Oxford University Press, 1977.

The Pentateuch and Haftorahs. J.H. Hertz, ed. London: Soncino Press, 1978. (Includes commentary)

Tanakh. Philadelphia: The Jewish Publication Society of America, 1988. (Highly recommended)

Plaut, W. Gunther; Bamberger, Bernard J.; and Hallo, William W. *The Torah: A Modern Commentary*. New York: The Union of American Hebrew Congregations, 1981. (Includes commentary and is highly recommended)

About Midrash

Holtz, Barry W., ed. "Midrash." In *Back to the Sources*. New York: Summit Books, 1984.

"Midrash." In *Encyclopaedia Judaica*. Jerusalem: Keter Publishing House Jerusalem Ltd., 1972.

Porton, Gary G. *Understanding Rabbinic Midrash*. Hoboken, NJ: KTAV Publishing House, 1985.

Classical Midrash

The Midrash. H. Friedman and Maurice Simon, eds. London: Soncino Press, 1939 and 1951.

Pesikta de Rab Kahanna. William Braude and Israel Kapstein, translators. Philadelphia: Jewish Publication Society, 1975.

Pesikta Rabbati. William Braude, translator. New Haven: Yale University Press, 1968.

Pirkei de Rebbe Eliezar. Gerald Friedlander, translator and annotator. New York: Sepher-Hermon Press, 1916.

Tanna Debe Eliyyahu. William Braude and Israel Kapstein, translators. Philadelphia: Jewish Publication Society, 1981.

Collections of Classical Midrash

Bialik, Hayyim Nahman, and Rawnitzky, Yehoshua Hana. *Sefer Ha-aggadah*. Selected, annotated, and translated by Chaim Pearl. Tel Aviv: Dvir Publishing House, 1988.

Ginzberg, Louis. *Legends of the Jews*. Philadelphia: The Jewish Publication Society of America, 1909–1968. 7 volumes.

Glatzer, Nahum N. *Hammer on the Rock*. New York: Schocken, 1962.

Modern Approaches

Loeb, Sorel Goldberg, and Kadden, Barbara Binder. *Teaching Torah: A Treasury of Insights and Activities*. Denver: Alternatives in Religious Education, Inc., 1984.

Waskow, Arthur. *Godwrestling*. New York: Schocken, 1978.

Wiesel, Elie. *Five Biblical Portraits*. Notre Dame: Notre Dame Press, 1981.

Wiesel, Elie. *Messengers of God*. New York: Random House, 1976.

Sources Related To Midrash

Sources for Books in this Section

Behrman House
235 Watchung Avenue
West Orange, NJ 07052

J. Levine
5 W. 30th Street
New York, NY 10001

Sources Related To Dance

General

Editors of *Dance Magazine*, and Manor, Giora. *The Gospel According to Dance*. New York: St. Martin's Press, 1980.

Kirstein, Lincoln, et al. *The Classic Ballet: Basic Technique and Terminology*. New York: Alfred A. Knopf, 1977.

Martin, John. *Introduction to the Dance*. Brooklyn: Dance Horizons, 1967.

Educational

H'Doubler, Margaret N. *Dance: A Creative Art Experience*. 2nd Ed. Madison: University of Wisconsin Press, 1966.

Jones, Genevieve. *Seeds of Movement*, Vol. I. Pittsburgh: Volkwein Brothers, Inc, 1971. (117 Sandusky Street, Pittsburgh, PA 15212)

Laban, Rudolf. *Modern Educational Dance*. 2nd Ed. London: Macdonald & Evans, 1963.

Mettler, Barbara. *Materials of Dance as a Creative Activity*. Tucson, AZ: Mettler Studios, 1960. (3131 N. Cherry Ave., Tucson, Arizona 85719)

Nateman, Evelyn. "Dance as a Classroom Technique for Teaching Bible, Siddur and Literature." In *The Jewish Teachers Handbook*, Vol. II. Audrey Friedman Marcus, ed. Denver: Alternatives in Religious Education, 1986.

Choreography

Graham, Martha. *The Notebooks of Martha Graham*. New York: Harcourt Brace Jovanovich, Inc., 1973.

Horst, Louis, and Russell, Carroll. *Modern Dance Forms in Relation to Other Modern Arts*. San Francisco: Impulse Publications, 1961.

Humphrey, Doris. *The Art of Making Dances*. New York: Random House, 1959.

Turner, Margery J. *New Dance: Approaches to Nonliteral Choreography*. Pittsburgh: University of Pittsburgh Press, 1971.

Sources for Books in This Section

The Ballet Shop
1887 Broadway
New York, NY 10023

Hortor Products (also good for recorded music)
159 Franklin Turnpike
Waldwick, NJ 07463

About the Authors

JoAnne Tucker trained at Juilliard and at the Martha Graham School of Contemporary Dance. Ms. Tucker also has a Ph. D. in Theatre from the University of Wisconsin. She is the artistic director of Avodah Dance Ensemble where her pathfinder work of creating a modern dance company with a Jewish repertoire (and various published studies) has had a ripple effect on other spiritual belief systems.

Susan Freeman was ordained as a Rabbi in 1989 after studying at the Hebrew Union College-Jewish Institute of Religion. She continues her dance training in New York and worked as a principal dancer of Avodah Dance Ensemble in 1988.

Open Road Integrated Media is a digital publisher and multimedia content company. Open Road creates connections between authors and their audiences by marketing its ebooks through a new proprietary online platform, which uses premium video content and social media.

Videos, Archival Documents, and New Releases

Sign up for the Open Road Media newsletter and get news delivered straight to your inbox.

Sign up now at
www.openroadmedia.com/newsletters

FIND OUT MORE AT
WWW.OPENROADMEDIA.COM

FOLLOW US:
@openroadmedia and
Facebook.com/OpenRoadMedia

www.ingramcontent.com/pod-product-compliance
Lightning Source LLC
Chambersburg PA
CBHW030231170426
43201CB00006B/176